The Lonely
Tumbling Waters

To Valerie

A book about Roe deer
and things,

Ken

The Lonely Tumbling Waters

Ken Griffin

authorHOUSE®

AuthorHouse™
1663 Liberty Drive
Bloomington, IN 47403
www.authorhouse.com
Phone: 1-800-839-8640

First published by AuthorHouse   11/19/2011

ISBN: 978-1-4678-8692-5 (sc)
ISBN: 978-1-4678-8693-2 (ebk)

Printed in the United States of America

CONTENTS

Introduction

I never knew my grandparents because the First World War had taken its toll and they were long-gone before I was born. Perhaps some bruised memories were too raw for my parents to dwell upon so the subject of their immediate past was subconsciously buried. Very little, therefore, was ever said about my grandparents and I have only the sketchiest account of their existence.

John Fowler, my mother's father, was from Kelty which was a mining community in Fife. He had joined his local regiment, the Black Watch, and died from the effects of mustard gas shortly after his return from the First World war.

My father's father, and here I realise that I don't even know his first name, was a second generation Irish-Australian who joined the Australian Army during the same war. He met and married an English girl whom he met whilst on detachment to London.

Her family were friends of his relations in Hendon which I am told was a village outside London in those days, and my father was born whilst grandfather was back with his regiment, 'doing his bit'.

After the war ended he returned to England in order to rejoin his family, but it appears that he was something of a restless soul as he disappeared and the last traces of him ended in Cairo.

Thus my father was brought up by relations as his mother then decided to desert him and ironically, she married a judge and they went off to live in Australia.

I decided, therefore, that this trend should not continue on to the next generation. Times have been changing rapidly since I came into this world and it became obvious that the reality of my existence and that of my immediate elders would soon be lost and forgotten unless I did something about it.

When I mentioned my intention to a friend it was emphasised that I should go ahead with an account of those years, but that the story should also be published for the interest of others. Thus what you are about to read was, in the beginning, a form of story letter to my grandchildren so I make no apologies for my ramblings.

I have never been ambitious in the common sense of the word, and there are some things which I leave until the time 'feels right', then one day I will have picked up a tool and be engrossed in a project which will occupy my mind to the exception of other things. This is a form of laziness I suppose, and it includes a reluctance to push myself forward or strut into the limelight, but on the physical side I always seem to be busy.

I have, however, occasionally found myself, despite my instinctive desire to lead a peaceful life, engaged in ruffling the feathers of those, who for some reason, appoint themselves to order the lives of others, but youthful idealism has, with the passage of time, been moderated to a degree by a certain amount of mature caution although my idealistic and somewhat spiritual nature tends to prod me on.

I cannot claim to have sat on the crest of a wave or ridden a star, but it is however, necessary to re-explore parts of my life in order to explain the environment and those within it which influenced my earlier years amongst a Bygone culture before I entered an increasingly convoluted world.

Friends have encouraged me to relate some of my experiences, largely I suspect, as a result of being anaesthetised by my contributions to *Stalking Magazine* over the years. It is, however, because of their urgings that some insights from a past age might be recorded. I was singularly fortunate to have been introduced to a wide variety of practical skills throughout my young life, and none of these except common civility, good manners and honesty, were to do with social niceties. My dealings with animals however were mostly instinctive, and have taught me three essential facts. They either like you, are indifferent, or distrust you. They have little artifice or stratagem other than that of finding a warm place to shelter and enough food to eat in order to survive and procreate, and in retrospect, my life would have been a lot simpler if the human beings I moved amongst had all been so innocent in their requirements.

Of my friends, there are two who have a thorough professional insight into the wordsmithing world; Susie Wakeham Dawson—nee Gibbs, and Anita Mason. I am in their debt for scrutinising and picking up on occasional over-embellishment, punctuation and my clumsy finger-jabbing spelling mistakes. To my friend and wildlife artist, Andrew Warrington who has worked on depicting such a wonderful cover and sketches—I thank him. It is at this stage in life that I am aware that I walk amongst some extremely talented and truly kind people.

So, to my friends—who know who they are—and to the special people in my life who help prop my feet of clay, I proffer my thanks for patience and advice. To my wife, Gwendy, and daughters Kathleen, Ruth and Eilidh, I can only express a hope that our present loving friendship is some solace for the earlier years whilst I grew up, and to those who have continually encouraged me in recording these random thoughts and memories, my thanks and, may I say it at long last, my love.

To the well-behaved youngsters who work hard and have little,
but who contribute to the backbone of our future nation.
They are, sadly, seldom recognised or rewarded.

The Woodland Sprite

Two dog-like barks echoed through the gloom cast by the tall conifers, and the young boy stilled to watch and listen. He moved his head in order to locate the direction from which the sound came, and another two hoarse coughs broke the cathedral-like hush. They were nearer this time, but still eerily resonant in what felt to be a timeless silence. These startling interruptions to the needle-carpeted peace of the forest floor, previously unbroken except for the very occasional muted bird call, were closing in on the youngster's position fairly quickly, and he felt excitement as he pictured the bounding animal leaping down through the Douglas fir towards the base of the glen. It was there by the river Endrick, in the subdued light afforded by the unbroken wall of conifers, that birch, hazel and alders cloaked the green river banks above the spate-washed boulders. The quiet air was heavy with the scent of earth and moss, and among the moss-draped rocks, wild flowers and delicate blades of grass gave the promise of another season, and a reason for buck fever.

It took but a few more deep breaths before the roebuck leapt into view and halted. He stood poised, a sprightly vision of russet-coated muscle, elfin-like in the rays of blue light which pierced the thick cover against the umber-hued backdrop of large fir trunks.

By the movement of his ears and fixed stare of searching eyes the buck probably sensed that he was not alone, but his mind was on other things besides a small boy in work-worn garments of drab grey, and with a bound he was off again, leaping high above the fallen underbrush, springing sideways and downwards in a seemingly timeless and careless fashion.

Infected by this show of uninhibited skill, the boy, excited and unwilling to relinquish this vision of unconscious freedom, turned to emulate the little buck as best he could. He was wistfully aware that he could not enjoy the companionship and trust of this woodland sprite, but for a short time they raced on a parallel course, gravity and taut fitness lending wings to the lad until the inevitable happened. His landing foot found a slimy root and he fell headlong amongst rasping dead boughs.

Winded and with eyes closed, there was a tentative mental examination of each limb and scratch, whilst the departing barks, now seemingly tinged with a mocking note, faded off into the distance.

This is but one small memory from a boyhood which I now view with some nostalgia, the atmosphere of which I would find difficult to pass onto my grandchildren because time and circumstances have changed so much in the intervening years that trying to convey the reality of my 'then' to a 'now', to minds conditioned by today's technological age might be likened to an attempt at transposing feelings of real belly hunger to a person suffering from chronic overindulgence.

For me, such happenings were commonplace whilst scouting about, marking future hazel fishing rods, or casting with those same rods, my many knotted line between overhanging boughs.

In the sepia-hued afternoons of warm summer dog days, empty nymph cases of stone-flies clung to bleached rocks like miniature primeval creatures, and dancing clouds of sunlit sedge flies presented obstacles through which my line wafted in order to gain those hazel-shaded corners which would sometimes yield an eight inch trout.

Hunting by snare or trap was not a pastime, nor in our case a form of pest control but a necessity of survival, and because the properties of some plants were still common knowledge among country folk, a number were used for culinary or medicinal applications. Everyone sees through the same glass differently, and I recall the realities of life as I saw them, etched in varying hues by characters of a bygone age. After the naïve atmosphere of the remote Highland primary school in which I spent my first few years I found the world to be unhappily complex and it was therefore not until I approached middle age, that I became aware of the manner in which I had come to terms with my physical and mental outlook as I moved through my life's experiences amongst nature.

Life Changes

During my school years a multitude of experiences were to pass my way, and like many a youngster, some of that time was spent in the freshness of discovery and dreaming. I sometimes looked westwards towards the dark loom of the great hills and passes which lay around Glen Affric, which because of their interconnected skyline profile were known locally as the sleeping warrior, and according to my father, cairngorm stones could be found there. This item of information added to my childish imagination as I surveyed the distant haze-veiled mountains where gemstones might be found and it lent a Tolkein air of mystery to a world full of wondrous things, thus adding to my preoccupation and somewhat solemn nature which prompted my father to nickname me 'the minister'.

I was the eldest child, and although more wiry than muscular in build, I had been fashioned by my father in stamina and skill. I was also the least adept at 'swinging the lead', and being the eldest I was his partner and workhorse during weekend wood-cutting tasks when he was at home, but my quietness did not always sit well with my father who was more diverted by the unbridled roguishness shown by my younger brother who had a way of easing himself out of any task or situation which he deemed unsuitable.

Eighteen months after the cessation of the Second World War my father returned from Norway. He had been sent there before my mother realised that she was 'with child' and this belated meeting involved some radical changes in what had heretofore been a household dominated by females.

During 1944 my mother had left the ATS (the womens' army service) and taken up lodgings in Chatham whilst my father was away. Owing to the circumstances it was impossible for her to remain on duty in that condition so she found lodgings and did what she could.

According to her—it was during the night of 18th February 1945 that she lay in bed listening to the throb of Hitler's doodlebugs (flying bombs), coming overhead, when she heard the throbbing cease, followed by a whistle and the blast as the end of the street was blown out.

Thus I was rudely born into a rather unwelcoming world of sirens and chaos, but I was informed that the wartime shortages during the next year and a bit of my life were alleviated by the fussing of my eldest half-sister, her husband-to-be, and his friends from the Navy who, like conjurers, were somehow able to produce lots of nice things from their hats, but things were to change. My father's delayed return in 1946 found me old enough to be weaned from nappies to that good old commode known as the pottie and I was sitting on that place of learning and doing my belated best to keep Britain green and the land girls in a job, when the backdoor opened and, according to my mother, this strange man with a stern face walked in and barked something to the effect that I should not be sitting in the kitchen in that particular mode.

The statement was directed towards my mother who was probably not too impressed with this re-entry of her male partner into her life, but my father's disembarkation from the troop ship had been delayed—of all things—by a dock workers' strike, and he was just a trifle disgruntled. He declared in later years that he could have cheerfully pointed a Bren gun over the side and given the fatherless sons a burst.

This rather negative welcome onto his home soil signalled a culture change from the austerity he had witnessed as a soldier still serving in post-war Scandinavia, and despite the circumstances in a heavily-bombed Britain which was already in the process of being tidied up, the drawbacks must have seemed relatively mundane to my father.

The cold reality of a return to civilian bureaucracy after the immediacy of decision required in the services rudely tempered dreams of the free future which he and his contemporaries had struggled for, and this often demolished hopes which had been raised by the end of hostilities. Thus my earliest introduction to my father introduced an entrenched habit of rejection and stoicism which was once again passed from one generation to another.

In the muddle of intervening infant years until our family moved to the north I remember, amongst others, a number of incidents which stood out in my memory.

The first was when I was just over two years old, and I recall the labyrinth of bombed ruins and derelict brick buildings through which I wandered, naked except for a vest. I was cold, sore of foot, lost, hungry and apprehensive, and I searched my way out of what appeared to be endless piles of brick rubble, nettles and fireweed in order to find the solace of another human being whilst my feet burned with stings and the abrasion from blasted brickwork.

I had been 'borrowed' by some gypsies who took me away, stripped me bare for my clothing, then in the morning, set me free to wander in the city ruins, longing to find some human presence until I toddled out into an area where I was noticed and taken care of.

Tall yellow-spoked wooden wheels. The smell of wood-smoke, the wooden steps up to the rear of the traditional caravan and the smell of horses. These sensations were embedded in my memory forever and my mother when exasperated, often exclaimed that she was not sure if the correct child had been returned to her.

The second incident was when I was about three and a bit. We were down at the seaside for the day, somewhere near Hythe I think, and I joined a group of young men who were diving off the sea wall.

The water was invitingly streaked with the yellow lines of reflected light, dancing over the rounded stones, and the young men were having such fun, when I mistakenly thought that I saw my father dive in as well so with no more ado, I adopted the diver's stance and plunged off the wall. I can remember the yellow lines on the stones passing before my eyes, the difficulty in breathing, then nothing else.

It turned out that my father was not with us that day, and I was lucky that one of the fellows noticed my predicament, fished me out and shook the water out of me.

The third was when I was considered big enough to be sent down the hill from the new house we were now living-in to another area of houses which had just been built further down in the valley nearer the Connie Banks. One of my age group was to have a birthday party and I had been invited, along with the rest of the country—or so it appeared.

Jellies! Ice cream! Custard trifles! Cakes! I had never before seen such riches and just like the other children I tucked in heartily, to my cost.

The food was just too rich for my system and I was very ill so the kind ladies cleaned me up and set me on the way home, feeling a bit sorry and sad.

On the way back up hill there was a level playing park and in it there were swings and a slide, and it was whilst passing unheedingly under the slide that a piece of brick or stone was dropped onto my head.

I remember the crunch and the jarring pain, then my eyes were filled with blood and I wiped it away with my sleeve whilst I carried on home, over the remainder of the park towards the last steep gradient; but life had not done with me for the day.

As often happened in the southern lands, a thunderhead had grown in the sky and the day swiftly darkened into a heavy gloom, then there was a booming crash as a sheet of light seemed to illuminate the world, and my already disrupted belly decided to empty itself.

So, I arrived back home from my first party with sick on my front, a still-bleeding scalp wound with blood over my face and clothing, and as for my short trousers and pants . . . !

My mother swore that this would be the last birthday party I would ever attend—and little did she know how prophetic that pronouncement was to be.

Then came the day which—after constant application by my mother—I was accepted into early school. A bread bun shaped like a real loaf cost a penny at that time, and that was my elevenses. There was no butter as that was still rationed but I seem to recall that the little bottles containing a third of a pint of milk were being issued to all schoolchildren at school.

I was very vague about what the teacher told us in the morning before class began as I was on the outskirts of the group and apart from being confused I didn't really hear, so I was somewhat puzzled when the afternoon school transport drove straight past the usual stop, but as none of the other kids seemed to worry, I just went with the flow and stopped my tummy from rumbling.

The occasion was one in which the mayor, a smartly suited man with lots of silver hanging around his neck, was planting the first tree of a new housing scheme with a silver spade.

Everyone was supposed to be highly impressed, but my attention wandered further up along the smoothly curved hill where I saw a huge khaki balloon with a basket going up into the sky on a long hawser, then parachutists jumping out.

So the late afternoon wore on and I got bored as the short attention span of infants is notorious, but what did catch my attention was that no one had thought of the necessity for ablutions, and I badly needed to 'go', so squirming and holding back because all of the teachers were engrossed in the formalities of assisting the mayor, I eventually plucked up enough courage to tug the Burberry coat of a seemingly mature girl and told her of my plight. A hurried whisper to her friends, and they pulled me aside then formed a ring of coats behind which I could hide, but it occurred to me in later years that these angels of mercy were all facing inwards! I was too busy with relief to notice at the time.

Then came the last Christmas we were to have in England. There seemed to be a lack of Christmas trees for some reason and my father decided to take me for a walk in order to search for boughs or an off-cut which might suffice.

It might be my imagination, but seasons were characterised by what we might imagine as real seasonal weather in those times and we had been blessed by a fall of snow (well at least the children had been blessed as the adults didn't seem too impressed).

So off we went on our epic adventure in search of the mystical Christmas tree, but struggling through four inches of iced snow became less fun and more of an endurance for little legs. We worked our way up the furrows of a turnip field where some of the snow had partially melted and I was quickly down on my face amidst the resulting slushy mud. I recall lying like a stranded seal with its flippers up in the air until I made myself push my hands into the freezing mud and stand again.

My father recognised that I was a little tired so he took a small turnip and bashed some of the skin off in order that I could nibble at it but by this time the romance of looking for a Christmas tree had fled to be replaced by a weary resignation because I knew that no matter how uncomfortable it became, the game would not be over until my father had achieved his aim.

Even at that age, however, I was driven by the force which was to generate much of my motivation for the years to come, that of seeking his approval mixed with an inborn stubbornness never to back away from a hardship.

At the top of the field I saw the blessed sight of huge Christmas trees. All conifers were of course Christmas trees to a child of my age, but when we gained their shelter I realised that they were much taller than high buildings and the occasional stunted one which my father hoped to find did not materialise.

Now the gloom really set in for me. I was tired and with numb toes. What did I want with a Christmas tree anyway? My sister Margaret was younger than me and she might not be bothered in any case, so I was more than ready to return home; but on we went in relative silence with the occasional gruff prompt from my father; "not long now".

At the side of the forest trail there appeared a clearing, and in this clearing was a large wooden hut which had been built on a raised platform some three feet off the ground; my father led me round to what I thought was the rear of the building which was facing away from the trail, and there was a flight of steps leading up to a door. The door was closed but from the interior of the hut there wafted the hubbub of voices and the delicious smell of cooking.

Ah! The magic senses of the young nose. We went inside although I was feeling quite shy, but my father led me up to an empty bench seat and table against the wall and sat me down whilst he went about his business of getting a warm drink for us both.

The men were jovial and ruffled my hair. They smelled of resin, tobacco and wood chips, and soon my tingling toes were cosy again and I felt sleepily secure amidst this rough friendliness. These were woodsmen and it was my first experience of male camaraderie.

All too soon the reality of venturing back outside came to pass. I vividly recall that there was a hard grey look about the afternoon and clouds were thickening once again. We set off for home but the route was mostly downhill this time so it was a lot easier for me, whilst the folds of my socks which had slipped down inside my little boots to my toes didn't bother me so much as I knew that the purgatory would soon come to an end. We arrived back without a tree but that festive addition mysteriously materialised nearer to Christmas day.

Some two and a half years after my father returned he decided to head north, obtaining work with the Forestry Commission in Genurquhart on the North side of Loch Ness. It was a muddled beginning, but here I was, transported some six hundred miles to a new location and reality, surveying the blue distance of the north-western Inverness-shire mountains. From my child's view of the world I had been plunged into the extremely closed social patterns of a Highland glen, and my circumstances had changed almost overnight as the north of Scotland was to experience relative isolation, economic and transport problems for some time.

Gone was the new neat house, as were my toys and smarter clothing, which strangely enough I did not miss. In place of all this ranged the seemingly endless, strongly scented, dark green forests of spruce, pine and larch, the smell of resin-filled kindling drying by the black iron fire grate, and dim evening light provided by oil burning wick lamps.

In this reality there was a strange concoction called brose for breakfast. This was made by mixing oatmeal and a pinch of salt in boiling water, to form a strong, nutty, paste-like porridge. A bagpipe practise chanter was thrust into my fumbling hands and I was shown how to adjust my fingers to suit the holes, and my world centred within my mind whilst it grappled with the enormity of this change.

This endless space was inhabited by strange but kindly folks who interacted in a relatively informal manner whilst maintaining a respectful hierarchy between the young and old, and this was complicated by a vastly different accent which took time to absorb, but unknown to my parents or me, there existed another space in my mind which yearned to be filled; the one reserved for physical reassurances and open signals of affection.

Although nothing was directly said by my father, physical demonstrations within the family were taboo, either privately or publicly, but despite this the secret void in my life, was, for a little while, filled by one of the most beautiful creatures I have ever known, and I believed that no one knew of it except myself.

This being had hair so raven dark that it shone blue. Her eyes were almost violet, and she was a year younger than my four and a half. We were the only children of that age group at the time; we walked and played together, and I picked flowers for her in secret in case my father found out and disapproved. Her name was Judy Nelson, she was in my innocent eyes, perfection, and we were playmates for an all too brief period before her family moved away to Canada and I was placed into primary school to once again adjust and deal with change.

A kaleidoscope of passing faces and unnamed people all mixed in with passing events which did not concern the minds of little children, filled the surface layers of my life for a while, but the wild quietly took hold of the deeper parts of me, and it was to fill that void which my work-weary parents were not aware of. This new preoccupation with nature must have made me rather difficult to understand at times as there was no language by which I could express myself even if I had been asked. Hushed voices contained within the music of babbling stream currents, and the booming and muting of life elements in the dim, overhung gullies where I plied my hazel wand after the darting trout, filled my ears, permeated the fibre of my being and fired my senses.

In the secret places of stream banks which had worn through the ages into the ascending reaches of the forests and hillsides lay the uncomplicated simplicity within which I felt reassurance. It was a straightforward situation of cause and effect and I was in no danger of mental or physical harm provided that I played by the rules. If I made a slip or did something stupid—I paid for it with a bruise or two, and so I learned my own lessons of physical and mental control.

I was not aware of it but before my schooldays ended and I went out into the world my body became as taut as a bow and my hands were padded with work-hardened callouses. I could run and leap all day with unconscious skill, and with a single blow of a sharp billhook, neatly sever a birch sapling as thick as a man's wrist. Three precisely delivered blows from a razor-sharp, four pound axe into the same incision would fell a four inch tree, and I was more at home amid the woods and streams than in human company. I had learned that as a mere human in a wild environment, and in order to equate with that environment I had to fly past any 'finishing tape' and only ease back at some point beyond.

Small wonder then that I gazed towards the Affric hills with wonder and dreaming, but then, there were a number of coincidental forces at work to create situations and difficulties in my future; not least because I subconsciously refused to fit into the average mould of things. I must have presented to the world a rather enigmatic picture, and in particular to those teachers who were to witness my passing through their lives for an all-too-brief period.

Taken from the adult perspective, I can see that our family must have been viewed with mixed feelings because of the number of moves, jobs and changes in circumstances we underwent. Such post-war fluctuations for new settlers was not so unusual and I was sent to no less than four schools before I was twelve. All of these had some sort of time lag in between, and each area had a slightly different curriculum.

One of the problems was the contrast between the entrenched Highland families and the incoming cultures. These quietly clashed as during that era, all Highland culture was steeped in Bible strictures of one sort or another, and here I was, a stranger from a non-churchgoing family who hardly fitted into the Highland perspective of close community and stability. I was reserved by nature, taught to avoid physical contact, and imbued with a fear of rejection. I had trouble remembering the 100th Psalm, but in the environment I had gravitated towards as my sanctuary I would kneel and quietly weep beside the body of a roe deer found dead by the riverside, and ask a silent God why it had happened to such a beautiful creature, whilst the delicate mauve-tinged petals of the wood sorrel bloomed amongst nearby mosses.

All in all, to the various teachers who were from the churchgoing community, I must have presented an almost impossible task in too short a time, because in the innocence of childhood I was bewildered that the all-seeing love of the God which accompanied me amongst the hills and forests was quite different from theirs which was selective and gave compassion only to those whom they thought worthy.

I had a lot to learn about the human condition.

A Country School

The Strathnacro (Valley of nuts (hazels)), where we lived during the period of my second primary school was a small loosely-knit township of five habitations roughly located in the central and narrowest part of Glenurquhart. The hub of Strathnacro was a small farm owned by a retired police inspector named John Wiseman, and the house further up was owned by Jock (the Yank) Macdonald and his family.

John Wiseman was a big, austere but kindly man who had served in the Black Watch at Ypres and other battlegrounds during the First World War, then survived to become a police inspector. He originally hailed from Burghead which was a fishing village on the east coast and, like many of his hardy breed, was a hard-working man well into his years when I first came across him.

'Jock the Yank', (Macdonald), and his family lived some three hundred yards further up the glen in their family home above a big bend in the main road. Jock's father had been in America, and Jock was married to a woman by the name of Chrissie Stoddart whose forbears, as shepherds, came north from the borders with the wool barons. It was these lairds who created the initial Highland Clearances by taking over much of the land, clearing it of people, and burning the vegetation and houses in order to create huge sheep ranches, but I did not know of that in my childhood days as it was of no real consequence to me except as a vague historical fact. I was to meet a number of Stoddarts in later life, and they were all connected by blood, to deer stalking and shepherding, and in some cases, amongst the top class exponents of the bagpiping world.

At the bottom end of the township lived Jock (Down) MacDonald and his sister, Det, who were not related to the (Upper) Macdonalds, and directly next door to them lived an old widow-woman by the name of Mrs. Chisholm who had a couple of boarded-out children in her care.

The Chisholm clan were based mainly from the Cannich area over in Strathglass which was over the hill north and west of us, and they were great cattle poachers in their day—although it is reputed that some of them came unstuck when they raided over towards the west coast via Monar and murdered a herding boy over at Kilillan when they 'borrowed' the cattle. They in turn were found out by the local Kilillan men who had been at the haymaking and who waylaid them after racing over the mountains. The Chisholm raiders were killed to a man and they and their weapons thrown in a bog.

But I digress. Det Down as she was known locally, was the headmistress of a small isolated primary school, the squared-stone building of which still stands to this day at Corriemony (Coire Moine—hill valley of peat), near the head of Glenurquhart. It is now no longer used as a school—and more's the pity, because some fine futures were launched from that humble little corner.

Whilst the methodology of the school curriculum might have raised some eyebrows in this day and age, my first years at school spent in that secure little corner were extremely happy. Bullying was unknown, and the early middle-aged schoolmistress presided over a unique seat of learning where the tides of nature were blended by her with highly successful accomplishments of the three 'R's.

Det had been born and bred in this glen where children of her generation and mine played key working roles in the business of eking out a living and it might be borne in mind that it was no mean feat for a female child from the reality of her male-dominated period to attain the academic qualifications required in order to teach future generations on her home ground. She and her peers took the cycle of seasonal tasks as a matter of course, and this endowed her with a true working insight into the Highland people, and in particular her pupils. It also enabled her to extract with sympathy the best from those children according to their circumstances.

So much for modern social work and psychology. Det was a bit sparse on housewifely skills, her energies being more streamed towards her chosen career, but unconscious forms of social care were an inherent part of teacher responsibility, backed by grateful parents and good old-fashioned discipline, and it was all being done with more practical application and sympathy before such things were pounced upon by self-important do-gooders who turned it all into a separate and often inept career.

Det produced successful pupils with only the aid of a few textbooks, a blackboard, slates, chalk and a lot of insight. Punishment for misdemeanours was corporal and dished out by means of a fierce look and a few light pats on the hand from an old case belt. This chastisement was feared, not for its pain which was nonexistent on a country boy's calloused hands, but because it demeaned the recipient before others, and more importantly, it betokened a temporary lowering of esteem in the eyes of the lady who administered it.

The girls were exempt from such 'brutality' in any case, but merely cowered under the weight of a verbal chastisement and their guilt.

The old case belt seldom saw light of day, and the pupils of my age group regarded this spinster with a mixture of guarded awe and affection. I remember one particular afternoon when we were told to clean our writing slates with damp dusters and clear our desks. Det had obviously been regarding the welcoming sun through the windows as longingly as the rest of us after a few days of persistent rain, and we were led outside and placed at strategic points beside the little stream which tumbled down from the hill through the birch trees past the school. This sternly humorous lady instructed us to remove shoes and socks whilst she did the same, then picking up her long skirts and tucking them up into the elasticated bottoms of her voluminous bloomers, bade us all take places in the various little pools which were calming after the spate, and demonstrated how to scoop a glittering fish up onto the bank.

With more zest than skill we all set to, and soon a couple of dozen beautiful travelling sea trout smolts were gathered together to be taken inside and shared between us all. This lady knew the smolts would be running down to the sea in plenitude, unlike the relatively barren nursery streams of today, and she also knew how to go about gathering a modest harvest whilst including a class of youngsters in this furthering of their education. We learned about why the fish were there that day, how they had to travel down the River Endrick, enter Loch Ness, then down the River Ness to the Moray Firth, and why we did not try to empty the little stream of silvery beings. The walls of the oak—and pine-lined classroom were festooned, during their seasons, with leaves and drawings of plants, and budding stems of branches sat sprouting in water vases while acorns and chestnuts pinned across the tops of small bottles of water sent white rootlings down and green shoots upwards. That classroom was full of wonder and expectant excitement as we never knew what would happen next, and during later years in different classroom environments dominated by the very real fear of harsh beltings, I often used to inwardly long for the peaceful little haven where learning was such a joy.

Because I lived just up the road from her home during my early teenage years, I often did weekend jobs for Det until I left to join the army at the age of fifteen, and her tokens of reward were as eccentric as the apples and plums appropriated off the overhanging branches of her trees were delicious. She was a foundational influence and a measure by which I set standards for other teachers in future years; few of whom measured up to her unassuming control and sense of humanity.

The Long Barrow

Very near the top end of Glenurquhart, some way above that magical primary school, lies an area of ancient remains. Of course the whole glen is as old, but it mostly contains the trappings of modern civilisation which mask other times. The Long Barrow, and others which have long been broken apart, including rubble stone pits from where much of the building materials for these edifices was probably supplied, is situated on either side of the old winding road, and a few of the children who lived right at the very top of the glen passed through these mysterious edifices to and from school.

We never played there; in fact, we kept well away from the place, and it is only now that it occurs to me that the dark winter days would have provided an uninviting passage for any individual with the least vestige of imagination.

No doubt there were other sites which could tell a hoary tale or two when they were still apparent to the eye, but it always sent a strange feeling through my bones when I viewed this place which bore witness to the reality that beings of an extremely ancient time had once walked where I now stood. They conversed in a language all of their own, but their children's laughter and cries would have sounded the same, and probably so too the inevitable adult bickering over those same infants who probably got up to similar pranks as we did.

The site, which to my memory stretches for about half a mile, is bisected by the road which cuts a path between these strangely uniform hollows with oaks and boulders, then emerges out onto more even ground where the long barrows stand. I do not really know where the exact site of real interest begins, but I always had a feeling about those hollows, and it seems remarkable to me that Scots and Celts from an otherwise superstitious race should risk desecrating such a site, never mind build a roadway right through it, but the influx of Christian religion set men to destroy much of what went before, out of fear, ignorance and bigotry.

As I previously remarked, some way down the road from the Long Barrow lies the first primary school I attended in Glenurquhart, and about a quarter of a mile below that stood a miracle of road engineering, one of General Wade's humpback bridges. This bridge, and therefore presumably the track, were built in order to facilitate the policing of the area by redcoat soldiers, so it may have been that the roadway route was not of local choice, but more of one who had little interest other than matters of military expediency.

Be that as it may, I understand that in recent years the old Corriemony bridge was washed away by a flood and was replaced by a modern one. This is a pity as a piece of history has vanished as well as an object of countryside character, but I have no doubt that a number of Jacobite shadows gave a cheer when that symbol of Hanoverian oppression disappeared. I can remember that the old passenger bus sometimes scraped her bottom as she straddled the middle hump, and the driver used to cross extremely cautiously.

I was a bit young to fully comprehend all that was going on about me when I was in primary school at Corriemony, but I do remember wandering off at mid-day playtime with a little friend, armed with hazel wands, brown cod line and bent pin fishing hooks, and forgetting to turn up until three o'clock in the afternoon to receive a real ear bending. The poor teacher must have been worried out of her wits at times, as we were very much swayed by countryside pursuits.

Another non-passable time-trap was a pond which sat just off the roadway below the old bridge road junction which led over to Strathglass. This pond was partly hidden from the road, situated almost beside the wooden garage which sometimes housed the old bus, and the water was occupied by miniature dragons.

Crested newts abounded there, and it was a real prize to capture one or two in a large jam jar, or better still an old-fashioned glass sweetie bottle, in order to re-create the pond in the schoolroom and observe these creatures. We were never allowed to keep them long, but were made to return them to their home after a couple of days in case they starved.

Nigel Ross lived somewhere further up the road, and I seem to remember him having an older brother, or perhaps it was a cousin. I remember Nigel, because on one particular morning he arrived at the playground with a strange helmet on his head. This was made of stiff, old scuffed leather, and it had what looked like very old straps of bronze as a rim, and cross-pieces which went over the top. Sticking out of the top of the metalwork was a sort of pin, and stuck on this pin was another piece of that dirty old bronze which whirled around as Nigel ran about the playground. The teacher arrived and Nigel was called into the school where the hat was confiscated and disappeared forever. Nigel had been rootling about inside one of the long barrows and had discovered this hat which I suppose must have been a relic of the Bronze Age or something of that nature. It would seem that the propeller had been invented for a long time and only awaited some form of engine to power it. We had no concept of the possible interest such a helmet could create, but if it once belonged to a tribesman of warrior class who might have been important enough to have been interred in such a place, then either these warriors were of small stature, or the helmet belonged to a young person of some standing. In a land where giants were said to sometimes roam, it would be no feat for a person of modern stature to be regarded as something of a phenomenon if that headgear is anything to go by. Nigel's brother also arrived with a short, pitted sword that morning and was brandishing it about until the bell rang for lessons, but that also disappeared. I suspect that some museum holds the items now.

The long barrows still stand, no doubt fully stripped of all recoverable items of interest, but their very presence lends an atmosphere of ancientness and the feeling to me at least, that one is treading on ground belonging to someone else. I can imagine the sounds of children's laughter and cries from all those thousands of years ago blending in the wind with the cries made by our generation as we too gambolled, not on, but within shouting distance on the nearby mossy knolls during our games. All gone and past now, like the old bridge and the school which is no more.

The March Brown

The parr and the boy

Darting and hovering in bubbling streams
of rushing sounds and fairy bells,
the flashing green of damsel flies,
and amber swirls in darkling dells.

Rippling toils cause shadowed deeps
to fade and clear like dreaming thoughts,
and catgut's surge sings through the rings
as grey winged flies flit through the rocks.

Splashing feet and bending rod
the hazel wand that bumps, pulls low
then silvered, twisting, gasping life,
dark fingered, crimson specks and so,

Reluctantly I send you forth
to dart amongst the weed once more,
and gain the deep of yonder pool
then seaward as the rivers pour.

T he first trout fly I was ever introduced to was the March Brown.
I was probably about nine years old and the fly was given to me
by my uncle Bob on the bank of a pool on the river Endrick.
We were sitting beside the moss-covered top of an overhanging boulder,
shaded by birch and alder trees, and I did not know it at the time, but
Uncle Bob was a pit manager in the coal mines of Fife.

He was a stern disciplinarian, and knew well his hard-earned standing
in life. This must have accounted for the fact that he fished his splendid

split-cane Hardy rods in collar and tie, complete in blue serge pinstripe suit and matching flat cap. His admonishments to me that I should keep well back from the water in case the trout saw me were accepted without comment until I had time to reflect on this anomalous behaviour later on in life, as he himself stood with ramrod-straight back fairly near the water's edge.

Aunt Bell, his wife, always seemed to time her annual visits to perfection, as these coincided with the ripening of the precious crop of strawberries which she and her daughter stripped and made off with after the interminable hours of weeding, watering and attention given by the eldest child labourer—me.

There was a reckoning though, when her personal Sword of Damocles, in the form of my incorrigible brother, Angus, swooped upon her one hot afternoon.

Angus was told to fetch a mug of fresh spring water to her as she sat on one of our rickety chairs, and because our pail was empty, he had to go to the well for fresh water (a task which he resented as always although he often seemed to have some excuse not to go).

In due course Angus presented her with her measure from the crystal fount, she took one look into the mug, screamed, and the mug, water and half-grown frog flew through the air as the chair toppled backwards and she landed with a crash on her back.

Sweet revenge indeed for a hijacked strawberry crop. My father was, of course, obliged to administer a fitting punishment—extra firewood duties, but in later years I understood that hilarity was poorly suppressed on his part.

On the fresh breezy afternoon of my introduction to trout flies, I remember being a bit disappointed about the drab-looking choice which was teased from a felt-leaved booklet of otherwise gaudy confections which excited my eye.

Expectation quickened and slowed as my uncle thumbed over the leaves of his wallet, poking thoughtfully at this fly or that. Twice he lifted out pristine models of grey and tinselled elegance, only to replace them, and my impatient perception of time had me fidgeting as the seconds passed. Coils of neatly-tied leader to fly gave off mysterious purple, brown and green hues, but this man was a master of restraint, especially in others, and I had to quietly contain myself as the rows of rainbow colours pinned onto rust-marked woollen felt were examined and dismissed.

I was, however, about to experience the utilitarian powers of a well-tried and proven weapon in the trout fisher's armoury, and the ensuing excitement as I watched golden and silver flashes made by trout and salmon parr as they competed for this morsel of woodcock feather and gold-ribbed fur will never be forgotten. I have a memory picture of the brown cord line twitching and flexing the tip of my hazel rod which hung in the late afternoon light over sun-streaked golden peat water. My world, suspended in that fluid of life, sang and burbled to itself through the narrows into the head of a pool beneath the airy shade of an old pendulous birch which arched over a huge rock, and will remain with me forever.

This new dimension to my experience more than made up for the lifeless glittering lures once again hidden from view in my uncle's fishing bag. His wordless choice of fly which was fastened to my old gut line with a turl knot, was the beginning of my education in the use of natural imitations rather than gaudy lures, and I was totally unaware that to a certain extent my life for a time was to follow in much the same pattern as either fate, or my unconscious habit was to place myself in life's fishing wallet as a March Brown, to be sometimes passed over by those seeking some form of glitter. I was, however, astute enough to realise that I almost always found myself among life's cast of flies as a reliable backstop and there were times when this seemed to pass unnoticed, but this was sometimes as a result, as I was later to discover for myself, of my retiring nature.

The Hazel Bush

Perhaps there has been a time designated for each of us to be individually introduced to the more acidic experiences of life. Some souls experience setbacks and mind-bruises almost from the beginning whilst for some the reality of deep disappointment or illness—hurtful in deprivation and loss—never comes until many years have passed, but of one thing I am sure, the hurt almost always comes at some stage and I am never sure if the gradual seasoning throughout life is less of a shock.

I suppose that it really boils down to our realities and the ongoing happenings we have experienced, but for me the hazel bush incident was a private, childhood culmination of always having to do without, or to make-do with cast-off materials which were altered and constructed for almost any purpose.

In the lean times when few of us had anything very much after the Second World War, this was nothing unusual, but all of us have our dreams, and my dreams were a bit above the home-made fly rods which I constructed out of graduated thicknesses of hazel wands, joined with short lengths of narrow bed rail tube and adorned with eyelets made from the bottoms of safety pins.

Wishing and dreaming is natural and because of this the reality of life can be borne with equanimity, but when the crock of gold is placed in your hands then torn away, it is a rude shock.

Many of us experience this from other humans as we develop from infancy, and this is all a part of the interactive learning process, but to have Mother Nature behave in such a manner—the single thing in my life which had never let me down as long as I played by the rules—now that was a different lesson.

As I already described, my fishing gear consisted of a rod constructed of carefully chosen graduations of hazel, jointed with narrow sections of iron tube cut from old-fashioned bed ends.

The eyes were made from safety pins, shaped and cut and fastened onto the hazel with ordinary thread which was then waxed or varnished.

Varnish took a long time to dry in those days and the wait seemed interminable.

The reel was an empty cotton reel around which the brown cotton line was wound, and the gut—then nylon—was many-knotted whilst my first attempts at fly-tying must have been a bit crude.

My fly-tying vice was a pair of eyebrow tweezers into which the hook was clamped and bound with an old shoelace. The tying operation was done with one hand whilst the vice was held in the other and this called for dexterity. Tinsel was virtually unknown, but fine copper wire from radio components provided the bindings and a furtive hole made by undoing the corner stitching of a pillow yielded various feathers whilst rabbit ear fur made excellent bodies. At least I thought so, and I caught trout.

But there was my dream; shining in the back of my mind. A REAL fishing rod. Elegantly tapered with subdued sleekness in varnish and bindings, and I had once actually seen a kingfisher line on an angler's reel!

Dreams are dreams.

One sunny afternoon in late summer I was wandering up from the river to the little cottage where we lived. My route was made the more interesting because I was engaged in examining the hazel bushes for a likely nut harvest as I passed, and also absently keeping an eye out for any likely growth of rod material.

Near the corner of the field—a part which I usually rushed past in my haste to 'get somewhere'—one of the bushes showed a promise of excellent nut clusters, and on closer examination I discerned the outline of a potentially nice-looking rod tip.

Now, I had learned not to get my hopes up as a wooden wand viewed from one angle might look excellent, but when viewed from another, might have a disappointing twist in it, so I restrained any enthusiasms until I wormed my way into the heart of the wide bush for a better look.

Good grief! I hastily looked over my shoulder in case a heavy hand clapped on it and a voice laden with the wrath of doom asked me what I was doing.

It WAS a rod. It was a real fishing rod, with bindings like rainbow hues and real eyes. It had brass joints, and I gingerly eased it out of it's hiding place for a better look.

It had a reel as well! And line on it. The reel showed little signs of rust pits, but no matter. It was a proper reel.

I again looked over my shoulder, half expecting some irate owner to come thundering along to the rescue. What should I do?

What boy could resist? I took a closer look amidst my euphoria and saw a team of three flies on a cast, all partly rusted onto the eyelets.

That was OK. The rod had obviously been hidden and never found again. The owner was long-gone.

My heart brightened a bit. If I gave the rod to the local Bobby he would keep it for a while in case someone came looking for it—then I could have it. That was the answer.

It would do no harm to flex the rod and try it a bit. The varnish looked a bit careworn, but I could sort that out.

With a flick of the wrist I tried the rod, and like the mummy in the tomb which crumbled to dust, the rod fell apart. The rainbow-hued silk bindings turned into fragments and weathered split cane sections parted like a banana skin and some pieces fell to the ground. The glue had melted away with time and weather. The reel was rusted onto the axle pin and the line was a coil of broken worm lengths when I tried to pull it off.

There was no irate owner to come thundering after me for stealing a rod, and the pivot of my young dreams; the one material thing I longed-for; had just crumbled away in my hands and gone back to nature.

No holy grail ever shone so brightly as that hidden rod when I first saw it lodged where it had been hidden years before, but it was not for me. I suppose that the person who could not find the rod was very disappointed and it would have been a great loss to him/her, but they would never have imagined the double disappointment created by it's eventual rediscovery.

The sun shone—but not so brightly. It was getting on towards dinner time for me so I put the bits back where they came from and left that dream to mature for a few more years. The rush of disappointment was soon replaced by a philosophical recognition that the materialisation of my dream was too good to be true, and I never did find out who had owned that rod.

The Glens of Earlier Times

During my wanderings as a boy I always seemed to slip into the same old trap of walking myself to the limit—then realising that I had to manage all the way back home again. There was so much of interest to discover—so much anticipation, and all of those things were just over the next rise.

On the intermediate plateaus above the glen, below the real high places of moor and hill there were long-established rows of large mossy furrows as wide as a town pavement on the top, and in nearby corners heaps of fallen stone rubble from buildings long-gone. In some instances the fallen buildings had been pillaged for the better stones in order to build new cottages or repair dykes and occasionally delving out new peat cuttings would reveal the stumps of old posts made from pine roots which were called sals and the furrows were termed as 'lazy beds'.

Lazy beds were formed by intensive labour. The ground or peat was literally dug out by hand and carefully thrown and shaped to one side to form these wide furrows. The depression created a drainage ditch and the furrow rotted down into humus and formed a place in which meagre crops could be grown. In the inland areas cow dung saved from the winter would be used as fertiliser whilst nearer the shores, seaweed was communally collected, divided out in shares between the families and used.

So many people inhabited the Highlands, especially after the cessation of habitual clan and nation-wide battles, and the next thinning-out of the population was to be during the clearances when the sheep barons, encouraged by the then booming wool industry further south, moved their sheep and their shepherds to the north, and literally drove the native people to live on the shores under upturned boats, or to emigrate.

It did not help that the policing, largely done by the militias at the time, was financed and practically owned under sponsorship by the rich businessmen and landowners, so the average country person had no choice but to bow their backs and comply.

Some landlords who were sympathetic to the plight of their people saw the imminent changes and encouraged, even funded their tenants to emigrate—in fact to better lives once they had settled down—but it was a time of hardship and reduced population once again. The way of life which had evolved in such a hard environment was created by a balance of nature.

Large families were born and many perished, but the hardiest survived to provide many hands to the plough, and life in such an environment was extremely labour-intensive.

There was, however, still a significant population in many of the more fertile glens, and Glenurquhart was one of them. When as a boy I joined the Cameron Highlanders, which was the Inverness-shire regiment, it would have numbered in all around a thousand men.

I was told that during the First World War, over three battalions of Cameron Highlanders were raised in the Inverness-shire area and that many of these men came from habitations which were scattered about the upper reaches of the glens. Most of the adjacent hill grazings were within several hours walking distance of one another but those places were now deserted and derelict.

In my wanderings I came across many of these places where people lived their lives, children played their games—when they were free to do so—and in the good weather the clothing they had would be spread out in the sun to dry and bleach.

How many little graves littered the landscape in those days? With the more modern trend of lining the walls of earth-floored cottages came tuberculosis of almost epidemic proportions, and in my travels through the miles of dark forest, I came across even more ruins and areas of what was obviously more fertile land at one time.

So much history, so much hubbub of life all gone and silent—and the conifer trees now stood sentinel over it all.

So I played the pipes and thought of the men who had followed other sets of bagpipes out of the glens with so many never to return. My tutor Callum MacDonald, in Inverness, was a Cameron Highlander piper who had been blown up by a hand grenade but survived to tell the tale and was then caretaker in Inverness Castle but he like many others are long-gone with the other shadows of the time.

So, if the lines of some of these tales might seem a bit sombre at times, it is simply because there was little glitter or vanity to be found in the reality of our lives. We had our contentment and we made-do with what little we could afford. Necessity being the mother of invention, we created many things out of old and discarded materials and learned to value the things we had because there was little likelihood of replacement. There was no argument and no alternative. Replacement just did not happen and *that* was one of the valuable lessons in life.

Ten and a Bit

I was feeling just a bit at odds with the world, although at the age of ten I had little concept of anything other than habitual uneasiness whenever I departed from my mossy environment of rocks, river and trees and entered the difficult-to-comprehend world of human interaction to which I was sensitive, but over which I knew I had no control. A cut or bruise could heal in a week as the blood scabs on my knees proved, but the years of schooling with unimaginative fact cramming ahead of me, for the most part manipulated by grey people who dished out punishment according to personal whims and religious bigotry, seemed endless.

These wordless thoughts passed through my mind as I stood on the road, calf-deep in powdery snow, and contemplated the two mile trek to my second primary school with the frosted powder billowing over the tops of my wellington boots.

The sky was a lowering dull iron grey and the birds were silent. It was so quiet that I could hear snow sift through the overburdened birch boughs many yards away, the hiss of feet moving in the snow, and the dull thud of blood circulating beside the inner ear. Beneath this frost-laden sky which was intensely nose pinching, lay a smothered landscape of pure white which was deeper than that which lay on the road, as the latter had previously been cleared at intervals. As a result, the off-road white was punctuated only by the black shadows of sheltered tree trunks and blue shadows. The bottom boughs of spruce and fir were depressed almost to ground level, and I had not seen much life sign for some days. Only the occasional stain of crimson betrayed where some unfortunate creature had been taken by an owl during the night.

There was a red-tinted ring round my upper calf where the damp top of my wellington boot flapped incessantly as I walked. Socks always seemed to slip down to gather in a lump at the toe, and that I suspect, was the wearer's price for a parent obtaining boots a size too big in order that one might grow into them.

There was another ring just above my knee where powdered snow flew between the short tweed trousers and my leg. Movement caused abrasion because the trousers were becoming frosted, and stillness caused the frost to stiffen the material and cut all the deeper once movement began again. I would have liked 'grown up' long trousers, but mine were hand-sewn from an old tweed overcoat, and although they lacked a lining and pockets, I was assured that they were excellent.

Gullibility probably still lurks somewhere in my consciousness—I think—but age has lent some measure of caution which is labelled as paranoia by those who get caught out. Clever stuff.

Two World Wars and a good old sense of British masochism had ensured uniformity of thought and instilled the idea that boys wore shorts trousers, even in winter. More sensible nations dressed themselves properly to withstand the cold, even the so-called 'backward' races, but of course I did not know that at the time. All I knew was that wellies were cold and constantly damp, and I had no other winter footwear at the time. This was my reality, and I did not think to question it.

There were a number of fostered children in the glen at that time—'boarded out' as they were known. They were usually outfitted with grey flannel trousers and jerkins which looked very smart and warm. Some of these lads also had tackety boots which were the envy of the others as they made impressive marks in the snow and smelled of sheepfat dubbin. It was fortunate, however, that I seemed to have no concept of envy, so quickly dismissed any longings. My rewards and reality lay amongst the nameless things in nature. My woodlands teacher was my father who was extremely familiar with trees and the use to which various timbers were put. I soon knew every type of tree and bush there was to be found in the glen, and by the age of nine I was fairly adept with a small axe, and able to help pull on the end of a cross-cut saw. By the age of twelve I could hold my own with a four pound axe, both in felling and snedding off the limbs. Keeping these tools sharp became second nature as I loved the crisp hiss of the saw as it sliced its way through the interminable firewood supplies. The ring of both handbill and axe as they sang cleanly through severed boughs was an affirmation of my growing strength, precision of eye and skill, and using the large Canadian bucksaw called for discipline of applied power. Branches and limbs had to be cut cleanly next to the sapwood in order that the sawmiller would not complain about snags in the milling timber, and as a matter of course, practising on firewood became a habit.

Text books did not exist in our house, so wild plants, apart from the more commonly known varieties, were just plants. I knew that some were poisonous, others could supply sustenance to a rumbling belly, some stung, and others alleviated that stinging.

Dried bracken stems could cut like a razor as could some grasses, and pignuts were dug from the moist river banks. These had a single fingernail size corm, and once washed, were a tasty morsel. Some herbs were also eaten from amongst the grasses, and of course there were crab apples, gooseberries, blackcurrants, wild cherries, hazelnuts, brambles, and the occasional small swede taken from the edge of a field. A sweet often consisted of a small paper twist containing a few grains of sugar with a fresh rhubarb stem to stick in it, and while it must have been murder on the teeth, it certainly ensured regular bowel movements.

Such was life for a youngster whose reality still focused largely on things around his feet. There was an intimacy in the close involvement of touch, taste and smell, and everything in nature was still a wonder to be further explored and savoured.

It was sad that intellect was stifled by my mother. Her childhood and circumstances in a small Fife mining community ensured that the long-term future of her offspring did not exist beyond their immediate earning power. This was her reality, but there have often been times when I wondered at the constraints placed upon me from one who was supposed to prepare us for the world. My mother was a hard worker, and her application to any task was vigorous and unsparing. She had no patience for idleness and would proudly inform anyone who cared to listen (often to our embarrassment) of any achievement attributable to her family. She had this blind side however, as anything outside her understanding was spontaneously destroyed or dismissed, and attempts to break free from this negative form of bondage were met with sustained resistance. In a paradoxical fashion, she had great wisdom and healing with infants, and her intuitive assessments of people were rarely off the mark. Perhaps my approach to the outside world was measured by my own expectations of how I would be received as a result of this, and there is little doubt that varying degrees of self-esteem, seldom seriously viewed in the context of social interaction in those days, undoubtedly had its own effects on the behaviour of my peers, my seniors and myself.

The 'Brickie'

My father's fascination with Gaeldom probably stemmed from his ancestral roots which were from Connemara on his father's side, thus his yearning was always for the Highland culture and this included the bagpipes.

So it was that as soon as my little fingers could span widely enough, they were coaxed onto a practise chanter and my lifelong association with the Highland bagpipe began.

By the age of twelve, after a number of years of tutoring, I was attending junior competitions and could extract various tunes from the heavy set of pipes without becoming dizzy from the effort, and it was then that my father began to send me over the hill to visit with an old man who had fought in the Boer War.

This old fellow was a stonemason to trade, hence his nickname—the Brickie. He was actually of the clan Fraser and his native lands were not so far away on the east coast.

The Brickie lived in what was originally a thatched, single roomed cottage, but the heather thatch had been replaced with corrugated iron although the earth floor was still in place and the old man had built a proper stone fireplace with a chimney at the north end of the room. For furniture he had a wooden bench and a couple of stools, a trestle bed of wooden planks and a straw mattress with some old army blankets, a table and a sideboard which served as a chest of drawers with a cupboard in it. His extra outside clothing hung on nails which had been hammered into wooden pegs between the dry stone walling at suitable heights, and the walling was sealed between the stones with mud and sphagnum moss.

So here I was, sent off into the late afternoon to walk the narrow, heather-verged hill path with the heavy box and bagpipes safely enclosed. I took to the hill from an opening beside the old winding road, up through some alder trees where, by the signs of widespread sawdust, there had once been a portable saw bench and as I walked I periodically swung the box from one hand to the other in order to relieve the banging against my knees.

The cottage stood in the middle of a small area of close-cropped greensward which was scattered with little heaps of stones. These had been gathered from the sparse soil as it was turned by the shallow foot plough over the years, and there was one stout and windblown tree—planted many years before—in order to keep away the witches. It was a Rowan tree (sometimes called Mountain Ash), and at the height of my head there was a fork in the trunk.

The single door to the cottage was weathered bare with age and the old square iron nails showed rusty heads whilst the iron latch—with no lock—was equally rusty, but the rust was polished with use on the hinge and the thumb-piece.

A small boy's eyes see these things because his height brings him closer to them and everything in the world is a new experience.

I would tap at the door if it was open or closed and call "hello?", and in the evening light the interior of the cottage would emit a soft glow from the peat fire and the wick-burning oil lamp.

After the fuss of the welcome and the mandatory questions about how everyone was at home—and if I had found the way all right—the old black, soot-covered kettle would be placed on the hob, and mugs and packets of tea and sugar placed on the table—with oatcakes and perhaps a little pot of jam.

Then the pipes would be brought out and the first tune the old man would require would be 'The piper's cave'. The evening would progress with music and stories—then a break for tea flavoured by peat smoke, the leaves of which were settled by dropping in a little twig—then the pipes would be carefully packed back in the box and I would be set back on the path to walk home in the moonlight, sometimes with clouds flitting over the moor and casting strange shadows as I dropped further down into the glen to meet the trees and the underlying darkness.

Thus I became used to walking in the dark and helping pass an otherwise lonely evening for an old man who had served his country in far-off places.

Post-war Wanderings

I n the period immediately after the Second World War, and even during the 'fifties when the building of hydroelectric schemes created employment in the Highlands, a man earned his living where work was to be had. The more stable forms of employment were small farming and forestry with ancillary timber handling services which, during those lean times, barely kept a family above subsistence level. Employment on hydro-electric schemes, whilst being more lucrative, meant that a man had to follow the work wherever it was located, and this meant family separation. It was also inevitable that when a person felt compelled to follow the goose that laid the golden egg in order to provide more for his family, the niche of more stable employment which he had left was soon filled. As a result, the breadwinner and family once again became itinerants if they had no established accommodation and local employment to fall back on. I had mentioned before that many people in the Highland glens lived just above the subsistence level, and this was certainly the case with some labourers employed by forestry subcontractors who generally managed to employ a few men. It was the case that income from their produce such as pit props and milling timber, had first to materialise before wages could be paid, and there were sometimes gaps of several weeks between wage packets. Their income depended upon getting the produce out of the forest and ready for the recipient, and their main weakness lay in the small size of their workforce which was vulnerable to weather extremes. Deep snow and weeks of iron-hard frost when felling axes developed chipped edges due to cutting into frozen knotwood made work almost impossible, and this often meant hardship. There was no romance involved in these winter scenes where exposed fingers were liable to adhere to iron and steel, and lean fare was the result. Any accumulation of wages was often spoken-for before it appeared, and to my mother, there was something psychologically damaging about holding a few banknotes in her hand, knowing full well that they belonged to someone else even before the pay packet had been opened. Although I was still young at the time, I had the ability to recognise the demoralising effect it had on her, and it was with great trepidation that I accepted any of that hard earned money with orders to visit the local grocer shop. My pockets never seemed deep enough to safely carry either the errand money or change, and I was in a state of constant apprehension. It was not unusual for me to walk the five miles home from school with a few bits of shopping from the village grocer in one hand and a two gallon can of paraffin dangling from the other, and I was often so hungry that I committed what was to me, the ultimate crime. This consisted of pulling flakes of bread from the ends of plain loaves where they had been torn apart. The bread was always served in paper bags, and even to this day my taste buds remember the dark brown crust, although my rear end has forgotten the price which had to be paid. My father would never accept any form of what he termed charity or assistance, and he certainly never knew that my mother occasionally obtained items of shopping on the slate. It was, however, because of the lack of work that we left the sombre shores of Loch Ness, and moved for a time to Leckmelm on the shores of Loch Broom near Ullapool where my father had gained employment with a forestry contractor.

Leckmelm was a small, loosely scattered hamlet of estate houses situated some four miles from the fishing port of Ullapool which was, in those days, still a small village of grey buildings clustered around the herring fishing-boat harbour. The dwellings in which the temporary woodcutters were to live were huts made from timber treated with creosote, and although my memories of that time are hazed with the limited vision of a small boy's realities, my life there was blessed with several learning experiences which were not to be fully understood until I was older.

One of my more vivid memories of the western seaboard, was that the air was spiced with salt and seaweed, and it is with recollection that I appreciate the kindness extended towards us during that time. They were of great importance to the emotional security of a small child in an area where comparative isolation meant that people habitually took their time in weighing newcomers up. Little did they, or I, know that before the next two decades had passed, the bells of change were to ring. Their culture was to be largely submerged by the bursting floodgates which found them unprepared for the negative aspects of affluence, and this sudden affluence and arrival of the more cynical elements of humankind which track the scent of money was brought about by Russian herring factory and storage ships, named Klondikers. Perhaps the lives of some of the more self-disciplined, older people were made more comfortable within the perimeters of long habit, but the rapid influx of sophisticated affectations brought in from already damaged cultures, were readily assimilated and mimicked by some members of the younger generation who were led by their incoming peers once comparative wealth was available.

So much for progress, but back to the Ullapool of more peaceful times. My introduction to this new land in the north west where great pink and red rhododendron blooms adorned waxy, dark-green bushes, was somewhat unique, and although I cannot recall our arrival which was in the evening, I do remember my first awakening.

In that period of limbo before my mind orientated itself, I awoke to a soporific sound which was so close that I imagined it was all around me. It was a regular rippling gurgle followed by the muted rattle of fine pebbles, and on opening my eyes, I saw a wall of brown boards a few inches away. I had some difficulty in collating these snippets of sensory information, because I had no geographical memory of my location, nor of going to bed. The thought process, however, soon got under way, and I recalled that the previous day had passed wearily in a cattle truck which bore the few pieces of furniture my parents possessed.

The unfamiliar sound came from high, spring tide waves which washed the shores of Loch Broom, the sea loch only yards away from the wooden wall I now faced, and I was torn by two impulses. The first was to lay and listen sleepily to the soporific chuckling sounds, and the second was to dress hurriedly and explore the source. In previous years, other waves I remembered on Loch Ness, had, to me, never been friendly. They were not tidal, their appearance was governed almost immediately by the winds, and they beat against the slime-blackened rocks without the gentle protracted sloughing movement effected by the seas. The space beyond the wave-beaten rocks often fell away sharply into peat darkened deeps which were inhibiting, and I gained no joy from those shores. As a teenager in later years I often sailed on Loch Ness in the company of my father. We did this in a sixteen foot dinghy which he had specially designed and constructed with occasional help from me during my periods of leave from the army. This boat was constructed mainly from local materials cut by axe and saw, and it had a large drop keel made from hardened steel plate. I learned to anticipate the difficult winds as they darkened the surface of the loch and gusted out of Urquhart Bay, and I had utter confidence in that boat and my ability to handle her. I always, however, instinctively disliked the waters of that loch, and the sharp steep waves which built up so rapidly. They were turbulent and unnaturally forced like the overfall when a riptide counters the force of a stiff wind. Perhaps the blame lay within myself, and I was not even aware of it, but many bloody scenes had occurred along the banks of that watery geological fault throughout the ages, and some had no doubt been absorbed within its gloomy confines. Its shape engineered the course of an ancient highway which crossed the Highlands, and I never learned to love it.

But back to the west coast and Ullapool. Adapting to a strange school was difficult, but the teacher was, in her own way, kind enough to the strangers who were to disrupt the even tenor of her class routine. I was, unfortunately, of little help because of my inability to ingratiate myself with those around me, but I was to learn the lesson that the milk of human kindness could spring from unexpected quarters.

Our daily routine included the walk home along the shore after the school bus had dropped us off at a farm further along the road, but first I always tried to visit the fishing jetty in order to see if the herring boats were in. Well-built boats with sound seagoing lines have always had a fascination for me, and I have no doubt that had an earlier event in my life steered me in the direction of the sea, I would not now be writing this land based account. Herring boats had their own special aura and smell. The black hulls, mostly tubby sea-keeping shapes endowed with black tar and rusting iron, smelled of a mixture of net preservative and fish. They squatted restlessly in ordered rows, jostling and creaking against one anothers' rope and old tyre fenders, with the wind rattling through the standing rigging, moaning like a lost soul. The men who worked on these boats appeared to have evolved as a humanoid element of the boats themselves. Their movements were purposeful and economical after the nature of those who cannot afford clumsy movement amongst lines and nets, and their conversation was held in the Gaelic which, although not alien to me, was without my understanding in those times when the language was fashionably discarded in most mainland schools. After my daily ration of creaking wood, staysails and tar, happily absorbed when the fleet was in harbour, I then visited the farm in order to collect our daily pint of milk. This was in a small, churn-shaped tin pail with a carrying handle and deep rimmed lid. These pails, in pint and quart size, were common at that time, and were often to be seen sitting at the roadside with the owners' labels attached. No one would dream of stealing the milk, as everyone depended upon the other for security. On one occasion I came badly unstuck on the way home along the grassy banks above the sea. Full of childish exuberance as we skipped and ran homeward in anticipation of our tea, I whirled the pail around my head and it slipped out of my grasp. Frozen with disbelieving horror, I watched the missile curve beautifully through the air to land with a dull thud on the nearest grass-covered sandbank. In slow motion I saw the lid ejected like a cork from a bottle, then the pail toppled over onto its side and the milk disappeared rapidly into the sandy grass before I could reach it.

Woe, woe! What on earth was I to do? A kind young friend led me to her home where she related the sorry tale to her mother as I stood at the front door. I remained stoic of countenance, as I had done an extremely irresponsible thing during hard times. I fully expected stern retribution, and I was mentally preparing for the worst. The scolding I expected for losing the precious milk was, however, much reduced, as the dear lady poured a tin of condensed milk into the pail then added water, and nothing was said at home despite my fears. I did, of course, admit my folly as I now owed the neighbour a tin of milk and it had to be repaid, but on this occasion the reprimand was of a philosophical nature.

Despite continual warnings, children often seem to need the certainty of experience from which to learn, and we inevitably got ourselves into hot water one evening. The water actually started off as cold, but that was the fault of imagination, interested enthusiasm, and stories of children paddling off to sea in barrels. Such stories were not unknown in storybooks, and we inevitably tried to emulate them. On the way home from school one evening, four of us discovered what we believed to be a sterling craft. It was the bottom third of a barrel sitting outside one of the fishermen's huts, and we dragged it down to the water's edge in order to have our first sailing experience. None of us could swim, the waves slopped about, and nothing had been said in the storybooks about the barrel having poor stability. The tub overturned as number four tried to struggle in, we all got wet, then waded through the seaweed to the shore. With the salt taste of seaweed and iodine on our lips, we left the vessel which had slipped out of our reach when it bounced free of our weight. It wallowed in the tide some yards offshore while we battered our socks on the stones in order to extract most of the water.

A few evenings later my forgotten mishap was rapidly brought to mind when on visiting the harbour, a gnarled old fisherman moved with purposeful rapidity in my direction. He was a stumpy figure with the inevitable short stonehaven pipe jammed in the side of his mouth, and wearing the universal soiled blue gansey and black serge trousers. His approaching lullaby went like this: "You'll be the young beggar who set my barking tub afloat in the tide the other day, well now I'm about to set you afloat too!" He was fast, but I was as agile as a monkey and slipped away at a great rate of knots. I have no doubt that he had a good laugh to himself, but my lesson was learned, and I seldom approached the jetty without due care and attention after that. I have no doubt that the tub, which was used for soaking the herring nets in preservative, had floated ashore to be retrieved, but it served to remind me that everything belonged to someone, and was not to be used without permission, there were always eyes watching out for mischievous children.

Harder times were to come, and my pastime of catching edible crabs with a piece of bacon rind attached to a length of string were soon to end. The day was to come when we would not be able to afford the bacon rind itself. The contract went wrong and the boss disappeared off into the blue with the wages and the men's cards, so my father walked off down the road to seek other work. My mother had made sure that he had taken the last heel of bread and cheese for this journey of unknown length, and we were not to see him until he appeared many weeks later. When my father did reappear, he had a new job, had earned enough money to move us, and had also found a house to rent. A walk from Ullapool, right down to Loch Awe where they had begun building the dam, and whilst a frozen winter with an empty stomach held no fears for him, it was another time of change for us children. We paid the toll of having a father who would bow neither head nor knee to any man, but work was available for those who honestly sought it, as long as a person was willing to travel, roll up his sleeves and bend his back.

He didn't get a start at LochAwe but continued on the road until he did get work, this time I believe it was at the Cluanie dam which was under construction at the time.

In the meantime, my mother with three children had to eke out an existence as best she could. Much of this was on a diet of oatmeal and onions fried together to make a concoction called skirley. We still had milk, tea and salt, and oatcakes made on the top of the stove from the same bag of meal made a change when eaten hot with some local jam. An occasional half loaf of plain bread found its way to our larder if there were a few spare pennies, but that had become a luxury. This was why the spilled milk was so precious and why I had been so fearful. There was little else, and we simply had to tighten our belts and get on with it.

It was at this time that an unlikely angel appeared at our door. Word had obviously passed in its usual way, and a character, locally known as 'Desperate Dan' called to say that he needed a lad to help out by carrying fish orders from his van to the houses of his customers. Dan was a fishmonger among other things, and he claimed that I would be doing him a service, but that he could not afford to pay me more than half a crown an evening. Half a crown was a coin valued at two shillings and sixpence, which was an eighth of a pound.

This represented a considerable addition to our meagre funds when one considered that an average working pay might be six pounds per week at that time, and so I went to work after school. It was, however, not to be too long before the lean but pleasant interlude on Loch Broom was over. We returned to Glenurquhart, and although the move meant a certain amount of change once again, our next main meal was a pleasant change from skirley, which I swore would never pass my lips again if it could be helped. Much later, during my army years while I was in Berlin, I stopped to have a conversation with a fellow who was groom to the colonel's horse. I found that he hailed from Ullapool, and mentioned the help we had been given by the local people. "Desperate Dan?", he said, "Desperate Dan! Yes I know him, he was one of the biggest poachers in the area. There was a good chance that the fish you delivered, wrapped up in newspapers, was red in the flesh". We both had a good laugh, but as I said, in this case an angel turned up at our door in an unusual guise.

The Iron Generation

I recognised in my father whom I idolised from a distance, a tremendous strength of mind and body. My trouble was that in order to gain approval, it appeared that I had to emulate his views of how 'right' men should be. I was not destined to have a frame over six foot tall, with shoulders like Cuchulinn, hands like shovels and a character containing all the attributes listed in Kipling's poem '*If*', so it was unfortunate that my father, because of unguarded and idealistic remarks made before an impressionable lad who yearned to be accepted for his hard won efforts, went and hatched out an albatross which hung around my neck for many years.

I was reared in an atmosphere where stubbornness ensured that just about everything was done the hard way. Favours were frowned upon, and I was taught never to ask for help. It would never occur to my father not to finish a job which we had started, and so the habits of perfectionism were imbued in a lad whose talents were diverse, but who specialised in nothing.

Good school work was expected, but academics were held in a degree of suspicion by my mother. Reading betokened idleness so I was brought up in a virtually book-less house, whilst physical contact was taboo unless done inadvertently during the course of work or play.

Skill in the use of work tools was held in high esteem, but in a paradoxical fashion, things like home-made wheelbarrow handles were left in the rough in order to be rubbed smooth by hands through time, and cuts and bruises were held in contempt no matter how deep they were.

I still bear the scar of a thigh wound which was raked out by a fallen barbed wire fence hidden in moss. I earned that wound in a karmic way, but that is another matter. On the way home from school one sunny evening I slipped on some damp grass and slithered on my belly down a steep river bank, the moss of which concealed the old fence. The accident was never reported because we would have been soundly ticked off for 'carrying on' when we should have come straight home, so a child's handkerchief was folded and rolled up tightly after being washed in the river. It was then inserted into the long rectangular gap left by the wire, and bound into place by a strip torn from my shirt tail. I washed the trench out with sphagnum moss and river water each day until a healthy scab formed, and slowly the walls met and joined across until the stiffness left and I could stretch the new skin properly again.

My mother never knew as the blood had been washed out of my torn short trousers, but I did receive the mandatory sorting out for ripping such valuable clothing. I remember that it was a curious feeling to be lying on my belly at the bottom of the bank among the polished grey stones. The water tinkled around them, and an uncomfortable rubbed feeling burned in my thigh and the heels of my hands. A hatch of delicate riverside flies danced and eddied not far from my face, and there was that low water smell rising from the drying green slime waving in the shallows. That puckered scar is like a photograph of the place where it happened, but the other children's faces have become a blur although I can guess fairly accurately just who might have been there.

My father was a great walker when he had the time, and this was occasionally done for pleasure during a weekend. I was always filled with quiet excitement if there was a chance that I might be allowed to go with him, and it occurs to me that if I had displayed my enthusiasm, these jaunts together might have happened more often. He also walked to work across the hill when the occasion demanded, and I remember him setting off on a Sunday afternoon to walk from Glenurquhart over to Strathfarrar and on to the Monar dam which was then being built.

At one point later on in life he told me that on his way to the Monar dam, after he had descended into Strathpeffer and gained the road up Strathfarrar, he sometimes met an old gentleman dressed in elbow-worn tweeds whom he named as 'the Colonel'. They would get talking and Dad would be invited in by the big old stone fireplace where—as Dad described—the staghound would be lying 'cleaning his cap-badge', and they'd pass a while talking over a wee small dram in the light of the flickering log fire before Dad continued on his way.

My father had been well-educated during his childhood but was a rebel and what was termed as a 'rough diamond', so perhaps the old Colonel enjoyed a chat with a man who had a fair amount of worldly knowledge, albeit encased in well-worn working gear. Perhaps he, in his comfortable old tweeds, discerned the value of the inner man and did not judge him by his exterior appearance.

My father began work on the Monday morning on normal shifts, carried on to work double shifts the following weekend, then reverted to normal shifts for the next week before walking back home on the Friday evening—arriving on the Saturday—to spend another firewood woodcutting weekend with us. Being just a lad, I had no concept of the enormity of labour involved in all of this, although I was no stranger to hard work. It was my task as the eldest to fetch the day's water in buckets from the well which was situated a quarter of a mile away further down in the glen bottom, and saw, split and carry wood morning and night in order to provide adequate fuel.

I also had to act as part time nanny now and then, and at the age of twelve I was no stranger to the delights of cooking dinner for the younger children on a paraffin primus stove as well as washing, cleaning, and feeding and changing a baby. A Mars bar proffered with a gruff voice when my father walked in the door after being so long away was a special treat, and it was a relief to have the security of his presence filling the house after the lonely responsibility of having my mother laying very ill in bed for almost two months after the birth of my youngest brother, Donald.

The distance walked by my father was something like twenty miles one way over hill and road, and to do this before and after a full fortnight's back-breaking work, rock-drilling and blasting in the tunnels, was no mean feat.

I know now that his latter twenty years of labour were spent with a hernia, but there was no way of getting him near a hospital unless he was stricken unconscious. A man who could still do a full day's work at seventy, and continue to odd job for pensioners afterwards is one of the remarkable commonplace accomplishments of that age. This was achieved by a generation who are now just seen as old people, but it was these men and women who fought for and gave us the liberty to live in self-indulgent ease today. They deserve honour and consideration, but a few of our latter-day intelligentsia, nurtured out of the blood, sweat, fear and lives which these people gave in desperation, choose to look down their noses at such 'barbarians' and some even go so far as to question their rights to defend their own country.

A Rabbit Screams

The amber of clearing peat water after a few days of rain, and the incessant gurgling tones of elfin music overlaying the background rush as the currents surged and eddied round the rocks, was a soporific sound as I wandered up the moss-covered banks, looking under stones for worms with which to lure the darting and hovering trout. It was not the fish readily seen near the tail of the granite pools which I was after, but the big fellows, all six to eight inches long which hid themselves under the miniature bubbling waterfalls where the tail glide of the pool above emptied itself over rocky shelves. I had to be careful though, and slip myself gently over the mossy leaf mould in order not to disturb the tail end Charlies, as they would dart forward and disturb the others. It was the sharp tug and throb at the end of the home-made rod that I was after, and the gold and orange speckled curves of muscle lashing in the air on the end of my brown codline as I lifted my catch from the mysterious deeps ploughed out by countless years of spates and waterborne stone, as old, or older than the fish species within.

From one of those overturned stones dashed a tiny streak of fur, and my young eye followed its progress to the side of a bigger rock where, after a scrabble of positioning, eager hands cupped this morsel of quivering indignation for closer inspection. The alarm scream of a rabbit distracted my attention, and as my head instinctively followed the sound, a sharp nip appraised me that this long nosed 'mouse' had fastened its minute teeth into the web of skin between my thumb and forefinger. This scrap of life seemed more intent on getting revenge than effecting its escape, but, fishing rod forgotten, and shaking the shrew off to go about its business, I trotted with my ears cocked towards this new sound, and soon saw the shape of a struggling grey form.

The creature in question was a rabbit, and it was near the entrance of a small warren which had been dug below the shelter of some old hazels. The rabbit was caught in that now illegal bread and butter machine of the times, a gin trap, and the plimsoles I wore, probably the cheapest of summer footwear in those days, did tend to get slippery with grass and moss sap.

I depressed the spring with my foot and the jaws flopped open, but in getting the rabbit free, my foot slipped and the trap snapped closed on my thumb.

What a fix. The pain ran right up to my shoulder after the numbness wore off, but I gathered my wits together, and after a couple of false tries when the jaws clapped together on my thumb all over again, I cleaned the slippery sole on some sand, pressed the spring open, and got that digit out of the old trap. The bruised but otherwise apparently undamaged rabbit had long departed before I could belt it with a branch (which for the larder, I should have done in the first place). So, leaving all secure, and the trap re-set, I got back to my fishing rod and wrapped the offending limb in soaking sphagnum moss. I caught very little after that as my mind was somewhat distracted, and the only witnesses of the little escapade were the waving hazel leaves and the rabbit. The shrew was long gone.

Nature's First Aid

Among my many childhood incidents which come to mind, was the time when an inch long, inverted 'V' shaped raker tooth of a large cross-cut saw was pushed into the inside of my ankle by a big log which had rolled downhill. This raker tooth was shaped much like a thick viper tongue and my ankle, now numb, was trapped against a tree stump on the steep slippery bank, so swallowing the bile in my throat and pulling my wits together I levered the section of tree aside with the handle of the axe I was using, pulled the saw out of my gum boot, and got on with the work.

A little while later I noticed a man cycling along the road above us, and I thought it was strange that he was coming and going in a tunnel of mist. I felt quite weak, but got on with the job and I was glad when my father called a halt for the day.

At his instruction, and to my relief, we each hefted a manageable section of log to the roadway and began the walk home.

It was not long before my father commented that it had not been raining, so I must have a leak in my boot in order to get my feet wet with all the sloshing noises going on. He advised me to empty it out before reaching home, and as I was a bit giddy and quite glad of a halt, I laid my burden on the grass by the road.

I then sat, and levering the offending boot off, I emptied a pool of blood onto the roadway. After explaining myself and receiving admonishment for being so careless in leaving a saw in such a dangerous position, I was told to pack the wound tightly with moss inside my sock, replace my boot by stamping my foot down firmly so that the boot acted like a pressure splint, and we carried on home with the firewood.

I ate my dinner, which I remember was mince and potatoes, and immediately fell asleep.

The jagged edged hole was quite deep in the hollow of my inner heel, and I had to walk gingerly on the ball of my foot for a few days, but youth healed well and left me with a mark which still exists.

There was a series of hard winters about the time of 'fifty-three, and these lasted until the 'sixties.

I was with my father one Saturday and we were cutting some middle sized trees along the side of a field near the river. Bushes such as hazel and blackthorn were part cut and layered or laid in the form of a hedge, and much of the hedging was done with the billhook which was kept as sharp as a razor.

Some of the larger limbs were cut with a Canadian bucksaw which was a large type of bushman with an extending bow held with a locking collar, and this implement was kept so sharp and well set that it fairly sang through the stoutest logs.

The snow was crushed hard and powdery among the trees where we were working, and the river had gradually hardened into a sheet of green-tinged icing like the top of some magic cake. All the stones and rocks on the riverside looked as though they were coated in glass, and elongated icicles hung from overhanging banks to meet the frozen torrent, suspended in time. The sky was high and silvery grey, and it was a strange thing this nose-pinching cold. The crust on top of the foot of snow further out in the field supported frost flakes which grew every night until they were over an inch in size.

I grew tired and hungry as the morning wore on, and my mind wandered to other things like the warm house, my dinner, or snow games that other lads might be engaged in further up the glen. In this childish mood of preoccupation I lost concentration, slipped and came down on my hands. The cold of the snow was matched by the numbing chill of the saw blade, and I saw the white quickly change to crimson as the neat slicing incisions in parallel lines opened right down my thumb to near the wrist.

I was duly despatched to crack open the river with the back of the axe and put my hand down through the hole to numb it. The hand had to be allowed to bleed in order to get rid of any dirt while my father got on with his task, then once removed from the green ice hole, some clean rag was bound around it. A strip of bicycle inner tube, carried at all times as an emergency axe-wound kit in my father's pocket, was wound round the outside to compress the wounds and prevent further serious bleeding, and this was tied in place with some fine detonating wire left over from his shot-firing job on a hydroelectric scheme.

Now doubly alert, I was put back to work. Time passed as it always does for a wee lad in a miserable plight, but centuries later I had my mid day meal while my father got berated for his 'crimes' in allowing me to fall in the first place. I confess to being a bit puzzled by this exhibition of feminine logic, whilst being slightly apprehensive about my father's reaction through being ticked-off, but he just laughed and went his way whilst I was given a seat beside the fire and a hot drink. The slight scars are still there, and that saw made a neat job.

Sunday Biscuits

The Mill Race

Middle life for me is
like standing on a brae
above a mill laide of my youth,
where yellow, broom clad banks
and moss grown walls
tell tales of times gone by.

Horizons lie shadowed, part' unseen,
and babbling streams
wash precious time away,
whilst music from torrents and calm places
sends drifting thoughts
through dreaming birch fronds.

Past drowsing noontide banks
where small birds mute
in shadowed brambles
and smells of mossbound flowers
blend in a rainbow of distant river sounds.

To the sill below the pond
where a last translucent glide,
reveals life's purpose,
and remnants of unsaid things
tumble in the fall
on the waterwheel of life,

'Neath creaking wheel
and muted hollow splash,
rainbows form and shadowed trout
defy the searching eye,
whilst time and water
both flow on.

Then tired, and done with the day,
like a tumbling autumn leaf,
my painful vessel returns to the whole,
and my learned spirit
Flies free.

Some times were better than others. When my father was absent from home in order to work on the large hydroelectric schemes which were sprouting like mushrooms in the Highlands in those days, the wages were good and my mother content. On the other hand, there were times when my father gained employment with local forestry contractors who were not always able to deliver their wages regularly, and this caused endless dissension. The pleasure of having my father at home was therefore tempered by other considerations.

It was during one of these leaner times that I was sent two miles up to the local post office and shop in order to purchase a packet of cigarettes for my mother and half a pound of rich tea biscuits to have with the Sunday tea.

It did not take long to cover the distance to the post office, and the cigarettes were placed in my trouser pocket while the packet of biscuits was carried in my hand. Up until then, biscuits had always come loose in square tin boxes, and it was a treat to be given a broken one if the person behind the counter was in the mood.

These biscuits were weighed out into a brown paper bag which was closed with a quick whirl between the fingers, but the new arrivals were enclosed in close-fitting cellophane. This new wrapper was to be the cause of my undoing in one sense, but my salvation in another, because on the way home I paused on a little footbridge which crossed the mill laide (stream), in order to look for trout. I placed the packet of biscuits on the hand rail and leaned over for a better look, and to my dismay saw them splash into the water.

With sinking heart I saw the packet surface to bob away swiftly downstream, and try as I might I just could not get far enough ahead in time to enter the laide and catch the evasive packet.

Oh woe! What was I to do? How could I go home to admit that I had lost the biscuits for Sunday tea?

Desperation now lent a hand, and dismissing all thoughts of racing the elusive packet along the stream bank, I left it to its own devices and cut straight across country towards the main river. I knew that the mill was not in use just then, and that the water would bypass the tumbling fall over the water wheel which would surely have smashed the packet, no matter how well wrapped it was.

Heart pounding with exertion and tension, I entered the stream where it joined the river and stood anxiously waiting. Had I been in time, or had the biscuits somehow wandered into some backwater I knew nothing of? Perhaps the packet had finally split open and sunk, the waterlogged remnants spread amongst slippery pebbles?

No, there it was, bobbing jauntily down the stream towards me, and with a careful hand-shaking scoop I had it.

Slithering and splashing towards the bank with my recovered cargo I raced off home hoping that I would not be asked to explain why I had been so long and how I had managed to get wet feet. The questions were not asked as the cigarettes were the main focus of attention, but a comment was later made on the first biscuit out of the packet which was slightly damp. The fault was musingly placed on travel and storage, but no harm was done, and the wayward packet of biscuits was soon eaten and forgotten.

A Wasp Byke

Sandy, alias 'Tom Doots' (so named as he nearly always carried matches because of his smoking habit which he somehow or other managed to maintain from the 'doots' of part-consumed cigarettes which he unearthed from behind the mantelshelf at home) was one of those characters who might be classed among the 'body part' consumer type. He appeared to be accident prone, but because of the rate at which he got himself into situations, it was little wonder that there was always something going wrong.

Perhaps his success and failure percentages were about par with others who found a less exacting pace of life, but I was one of the unfortunates who lived closest to Sandy. In a glen which was relatively remote in those post-war days, we were very much thrown upon one another for company, and when boys get together . . .

It might be imagination, but I remember being able to lie on the ground and still get up with dry clothes. Summers were summers then, and warmth-loving creatures abounded. Slow-worms, adders and lizards were plentiful, and so too were insects of all types. The lower part of the path to our water well was a favourite crossing place for adders, and many's the one I beheaded in my ignorance before I transcended superstitious fear and realised that these creatures were a part of the ecological chain, and meant absolutely no harm to humankind.

Wasps and bees were plentiful, and perhaps it was a sign of the prevailing weather conditions when I recall that grey globe-like wasp bykes were a common sight among hazel woods where they hung suspended from stout forks amid the branches.

Sandy's method of dealing with this sort of thing was either to burn them out with a tuft of dry grass lit with one of his precious matches, or aim stones at the byke and run like blazes but I was to discover that emulating one's peers can be a painful experience, especially when the emulation is only partly complete because of inherent differences in genetics, and therefore, character.

I had all the throwing skills, but a lot less guile than Sandy, and a well-placed stone aimed at a large wasp byke caused me no little pain on one memorable afternoon.

I was by myself, and the wasp byke had been manufactured uncomfortably close to one of my favourite fishing pools. I felt a bit uneasy about the buzzing going on as wasps had gained a bad reputation for stinging that year, so I picked up a palm-shaped stone and let fly.

The stone belted into the middle of the grey shape, and I observed in the same instant—stupidly remaining where I was—a black dot detach itself from the base of the byke.

The next thing I knew was that the black dot smacked me on the forehead just above and between my eyes, and reaching for the object, I removed a very angry wasp which was endeavouring to sort me out single-handedly and no mistake.

A brave little creature, I never knew if it lived or died as I hurriedly got rid of it before the tail could get busier than ever. I raced to the corner of a nearby field where I found a soft docken leaf, squashed the juice onto the rapidly swelling sting, and followed that with a cool pad of wet moss.

Lesson number one: Leave well alone unless you are directly affected.

Lesson number two: Always have a remedy to hand, natural or otherwise, if you cannot help getting involved.

Lesson number three: Don't stand like a dumb idiot. If you plant a natural bomb, retire well out of it at a safe pace. Most man-made devices are pre-quantifiable in their outcome, but natural elements are rarely so.

Lesson number four: When planning some little escapade, always remember that the success rate is usually minimal despite preferential memory recall.

I only implemented the second lesson, and a sore one it was too. There was no fishing done that afternoon.

'Other' Senses

Glenurquhart, where I spent most of my childhood had the reputation of being one of the most haunted glens in Scotland, and apart from strangers like ourselves who moved there after the Second World War, the main population consisted of people who had originated in, or had strong connections with, the Highland area west of Inverness.

In the case of our family, my father had a strong empathy with the Highland culture. Much of his own bloodline stemmed from the Irish-Scots from the seaboard of Connemara in Ireland, and my mother's people were from the Kingdom of Fife on the east coast of Scotland.

Although this meant that my own bloodline was drawn from widely differing areas, it was mainly of Scots and Celtic ancestry, with what must be a smattering of Norman and Saxon thrown in to complete the picture of confusion. I, nevertheless, fitted naturally into the rhythm of the rural aspects of the Highlands, although I spurned the restrictions, both spiritual and mental, of structured dogmas which many adhered to in order to remain socially acceptable.

For the most part, the natives of the Glenurquhart area were also the descendants of Celts and Scots. Their forebears had been converted to Christianity by missionaries who journeyed up the western seaboard and ventured down the chain of lochs in the Great Glen towards where Inverness now stands. They came from places such as the island of Iona, and whilst Viking influence probably played some part in the more coastal areas around the Moray Firth, no signs of their presence as far inland as Glenurquhart were impressed upon my childhood education. The local Celtic converts had, however, in a similar manner to the European mainlanders, decided that there was no harm in retaining little snippets of the old faith—just for insurance—and many of the old sayings included ancient bits and pieces which must have made the more fervent clergy wince with anguish as there remained a strong affiliation with such plants as mistletoe, holly, rowan, hazel, willow and oak, all of which stem from pre-history and ancient Druidic beliefs.

Another remnant from those times was the retention by some of senses which had not been blunted or eradicated by the dogmas imposed by science and technology, and there is more of the 'other' side in us than most people realise.

Hauntings were, for the cynics and manipulators, extremely useful psychological weapons but although, in the main, the local populace consisted of a strong churchgoing community, they were also steeped in superstition and a strong belief in 'other' beings, so tales of ghosts and strange happenings were legion, and hardly a month passed without someone having an experience which was difficult to explain to the more sceptical. It was also not uncommon to hear of people with 'the gift', and there were those special children, the seventh child of the seventh child, with red hair, who would have 'the sight'.

In a race with strong Scots ancestry, red hair was not uncommon, and neither was it strange in those days to know of a seventh child of a seventh child. Families were often much larger than they are today, although, before the dawn of penicillin based antibiotics and polio inoculations, there was of course much more childhood mortality. Transport was scarce in those times, and I doubt if there were more than a dozen vehicles in the glen, most of which belonged to the professional class and more affluent farmers. People relied mainly on walking or cycling, so the likelihood of encounters on lonely roads or hill paths, real or imaginary, was much increased in a populace which was much more in tune with the natural rhythms of the planet. Not that they probably thought about it in those terms, but the various materials they hand-worked throughout the seasons, had a special significance. They felt the texture and quality of what they were holding, and certain plants were still believed to have good or bad influences.

Everything had a life beyond a life, and utilising the physical part generated more life. It was not to be wasted or used without respect, but handled with thought and gratitude, to be stored away with wishes for times to come, which was why the older people placed so much value on the annual thanksgiving and harvest festivals. They were thanking their maker and the Mother Earth for her bounties without which they could not survive. A custom from times before our knowledge which, sadly, has largely disappeared.

I never considered either my family or myself to have any extraordinary powers, but of course, if something sits naturally within, it will not be counted as exceptional. I will, however, recount a few personal happenings which might give pause for thought, and the reader can place whatever interpretation they care to place on the subject. My mother always foretold when some communication would arrive from a relation, and she would mention several times that news was on the way.

We had no telephone or other means of passing on news other than by letter, so her insight was no coincidence. I too inherited that 'gift', and I also inherited the sometimes uncomfortable insight of picking up on vibrations relating to peoples' characters. I learned to my cost that timely warnings are not always appreciated, and also that "I told you so" is even more unwelcome, but despite this I was no more immune to fear of the dark than any average child or adult who has an instinct to get away from places which have no defense after the light fades. It is natural to seek security in some corner or dwelling, but like everyone else in those times, I had to steel my backbone, face the whispering night, and get used to it.

To stand quietly in the darkness with the silence all around, and wait while the eyes begin to take in shape and substance, is a form of discipline. It is even more of a discipline to take hold of those dim messages and translate them into normal physical actions based on trust of your senses and instincts, but this, with practise and confidence, can be achieved with success.

This is just another of the natural attributes which is becoming redundant with the advent of convenience lighting, and a natural laziness to use the natural alternative, but these are of course merely natural skills, aided by deeply submerged knowledge, and are in no way connected to hauntings.

Our family lived for a time in an old cottage at Strathnacro, which was about a third of the way up, and occupied the narrowest part of Glenurquhart.

The interpretation of the name Strathnacro, or Strathnacno, is open to interpretation as the open valley of the sheep fold, or the open valley of the nuts—which in fact contained many hazel trees.

This little settlement of houses was widely scattered, and included a small farm, and for several months during the winter, the steep hill which formed the bounds of the eastern side of the glen, blocked the sun from us.

There had been another settlement well up on the brae opposite us, and this had been reached from the other side of the river by a bridge and a now obliterated track from further down the glen. This place was, however, long deserted, and alders now stood in the deserted ruins of Learg nam Broc (the sloping place of the badger), where children had once played.

It was not until we were settled in to that little cottage that things began to happen.

The cottage was an old stone and mortar single storey dwelling comprising of three rooms, with a narrow lobby which led from the front door to the rear of the cottage where it split right and left, giving access to the other rooms.

The gable wall and chimney at the east end of the house was unstable, and partly fell in one winter, but my father rebuilt it and timbered that end. The timbers were then lined with cardboard boxes and covered with wallpaper. This room was almost always empty, but was given to me for use as my bedroom at a later date.

The main bedroom was at the other end of the house, and on several occasions my sister called in a terrified state to tell my mother that she had looked up to see a shape bending over her.

These fears were calmed and set aside, but some time later my father heard that a previous family who had lived there included a red-haired daughter who was a seventh child, and that she too had often witnessed a frightening presence in that room. My sister was not to my knowledge a seventh child—nor was she red-haired—but why should a young girl open her eyes and see something which terrified her?

My father was a complete sceptic, and always said that if something approached you and it was frightening, chuck a stone at it.

If it gave a howl, it was flesh and blood and the sensible thing to do was to run, but if there was no response, it could do no harm.

His education was about to begin.

Every now and then we would see a person in a light-coloured trenchcoat pass the window on the way to the door, and in the time-honoured way, one of us would go and stand ready to answer the knock in order that the guest would not be kept waiting.

The knock never came, and on opening the door, no one would be there, yet on many occasions more than one person would see this apparition pass the window.

Then came the Christmas we would always remember.

My mother was very strict about getting the house in good order for the Christmas dinner, and in order to achieve this on a single burner paraffin stove and the black iron range powered by firewood, she had to begin early. The children were always up and about due to excitement in any case, so our mother got busy lighting the fire and taking the wood ashes out to the garden.

In front of the cottage was a wide pathway which was flagged with stone. The other side of this wide path was bounded by a low stone wall, the top of which was also flagged with flat stone on which we often sat as it had been built to an ideal height.

Beyond this low wall lay a drop of some six feet or so, and the bottom of this drop marked the top end of the vegetable garden.

There was an opening through the wall directly facing the front of the cottage door and this led to a flight of stone steps, flanked by an old-fashioned, strongly scented burgundy/red rose bush, down into the garden, and about twenty feet to the left of the steps when viewed from the doorway, grew a wild cherry, or Gean tree which gave off juicy black cherries each year.

My mother went out of the house in the new day, in order to empty the wood ash onto the garden, and hurried back inside looking very white and shocked.

She had seen a spiral of light move slowly upwards around the cherry tree and disappear. That tree grew from below the wall where the original owners of the cottage, two old spinster sisters, used to sit and sing psalms in the summer evenings.

My own experience was no less disconcerting.

The water supply for the cottage, a spring well in a sunken shady hollow, lay about a quarter of a mile down into the glen nearer the river. In order to reach this, the main road had to be crossed, then a steep descent was made down a rocky path until the base of the glen was reached. The path then led into the hollow which was bounded by a copse of alders wherein lay two little wells in deep shadow.

The first well was where the water ran in and cleared, then it went through an underground hole over which we walked on rough-laid rocks to the second well from which we were able to withdraw a bucket or two of water. I preferred two buckets as they balanced me better.

I was sent down to the well one winter's evening in order to get more water, and I set off down the path in the bright moonlight which sparkled silently off the frost-covered snow.

Everything was fine. The night was so moonlit that no torch was needed, although it was much darker within the alder-bordered hollow, but there was enough light once my eyes adjusted and I filled the bucket from the icy pool then walked off home, passing the bucket every few strides between hands in a rhythm which I found helped to avoid arm ache and stiff fingers.

I was almost at the base of the steep bank, and busy working out how best to attack the steeper rise to the road by utilising the snow-bound boulders which protruded from the old worn pathway, when I felt the hair raise at the base of my scalp, and paused to turn around.

Behind me, about three feet in the air above the path, danced a ball of light.

It moved sedately to and fro, and as I watched, pretty well mesmerised, a thick cloud moved to blank out the moon, and the whiteness of the snow became a vague dim glow.

The ball of light was still there, sedately dancing about and advancing towards me. I turned to mount that hill like a mountain goat, and suddenly I was at the cottage door, bucket and all, but with no water.

The cloud cover had come to stay and it heralded another fall of snow. I was dressed only in my short trousers, shirt and pullover as I had only expected to be out in the crisp air for a short time, but the adrenalin faded to leave me chilled and shivering and I was afraid to go into the house as I had failed in my errand, feeling that my explanation would sound extremely lame.

Some time later the door opened and my father stood there. I had heard my mother's voice raise in query and after a pause the door opened and I was asked why I had been there for so long, so I gave a truthful reply.

There was no retribution and no argument. My father took the bucket and went to refill it himself, taking me along with him in order to reassure me that there was nothing to harm me. I was rather taken aback that they were not surprised or annoyed at my story, but the reason for this was later recounted to me.

During the previous early summer, my mother had taken us children down to visit with a relation in the West Lothian area, and during this time, my father, who was working with a woodcutting contractor, looked after himself.

He later told my mother that late one evening he was sitting quietly, when he heard a sound of psalms or hymns being sung in the Gaelic, and went outside to investigate.

There was no wind of any sort as it was a calm light evening, so there was nothing to cause a sound in the roof, guttering or downpipes. Yet still the low singing persisted. He investigated every possible avenue in order to ensure that he was not imagining things, but had to admit that despite his being the only mortal there—he was not alone.

That cottage and area definitely had a 'presence' or two, and one of them, the one which bent over sleeping children, was not nice. The other, however, was the one who appeared at the window on the way to the door, and it became usual to shout, "come in! Shut the door, and stop wasting our time", but the invitation was never, to our knowledge, taken up.

The glen was full of such happenings and premonitions, and the children who grew up there were never surprised to hear of such matters, so it was perfectly natural for me to engage in conversation about such things amongst my contemporaries later on in life.

I never lost touch with the knowledge that someone was thinking about me, and that a letter was on the way, but that can be put down to yet another faculty which has long been neglected by humans. The transfer of thought.

I think that most humans have lost the means of opening the doors to a number of their innate abilities, and perhaps this is a safety device which has evolved to ensure acceptance amidst today's society.

After all, it was not so long ago that innocent people with gifts of insight and healing beyond their time, souls who had the potential intelligence to break from ignorance and blind dogma, were being murdered in the name of witchcraft by a system which in itself had become the most bigoted chalice of evil operating in God's name. There is no doubt that such 'gifts' were not apportioned to good people alone and that this talent was corrupted by some in order to coerce and for gain, but as usual, the behaviour of the few became highlighted in the minds of the majority, and it is the frailty of humans to dwell on negativity and bad gossip.

Red Heather and White Flags

Sandy MacDonald and my brother Angus were much of an age, and both were as mischievous as monkeys. They were real con artists in their own right and always up to some form of 'smart Alec' practice. They were, however, not quite as clever as they liked to imagine, and witnessing them getting caught out or their carefully laid plots falling apart caused no little hilarity.

As I have already mentioned, Sandy had a fondness for the dog-ends of cigarettes which he unearthed from behind the mantel-shelf at home. He also somehow managed to finance the occasional packet of woodbines, and it was this habit of his which sometimes got him into some real scrapes. He was a terrible scholar, probably because he had absolutely no discipline and resented the intrusion of academic matters into his otherwise pastoral life, but his native bodily skills were phenomenal, and he could balance sideways on the saddle of a bicycle whilst careering down the road with his body thrown back and heels in the air, bouncing up and down and pretending to play the banjo. We did not always have access to tyres and tubes which were a bit of a luxury even to grown-ups in those days, but as long as we could raid a refuse dump for old bits and pieces, we would sneak away with our parents' spanners and rig up some sort of bike with unadorned wheels which ran on plain spindles without bearings, but smeared with lard, and down the road we would rattle, the height of pride and mechanical wizardry.

That was until Sandy got caught out one day. He was at his usual ploy of cranking himself down the road on tyreless wheels, puffing away at the fag in the corner of his mouth, when he saw his father heading up the road towards him.

Now Sandy's father, being what was termed as an albino, had better night-sight than normal, but was a bit short on distances during the day, so he didn't recognise who or what was going on.

Getting rid of the cigarette butt was difficult for Sandy because the paper had stuck to his lip, and in the scrabble not to get caught smoking, or playing truant, he wobbled and clanked at great speed off the road to disappear down amongst the bracken and scrub birch to an ignominious landing. Handlebars, crossbar, pedals and rocky terrain are not good cushions, and it was with a pained expression that Sandy regained the road to glare resentfully after the adult who had dared to place him in this bedraggled plight, his halcyonic afternoon ruined.

Then one of the annual charity collection flag days arrived, and children were paired off according to their home areas by the teacher. Each pair was given a sealed collection box with a slot in the top for coins and a supply of small bunches of white heather and tiny flags with a picture of purple heather, armed with a pin.

Several years had passed and I was away from home in the army, but the story was related in great detail to me.

Angus and Sandy were given a small cardboard tray containing the heather and flags, and off they went to do the rounds on Sandy's bicycle which, by this time, had tyres, tubes and even ball bearings, but had no brakes.

The usual way of carrying a passenger was to have them sit sideways on the crossbar, but this was not very satisfactory if one needed to stop without mechanical brakes, so it was agreed that Angus would sit on the handlebars and apply pressure with the sole of his shoe to the front tyre when necessary.

They had made some deliveries to crofts (small farm holdings), up in the hill around Rychraggan which was situated on an extended plateau in the hill above the main glen, and were returning towards the bottom when they came unstuck with the braking methodology. They piled, bike and all, into the rocky spate burn down below the road, and the tray of heather and flags, precariously balanced as it was, emptied itself into the pool alongside them.

No doubt there was a delay while they both decided that they were still alive and with all limbs intact, but it would be the subsequent dismay and scrabble for the merchandise which held the stage, especially as it was gathered hastily and dumped into the box before it all washed off downstream.

Two wet young monkeys with lumps on their heads and multicoloured, soggy heather and flags failed to impress anyone as salesmen, and the problem was compounded when concussion was diagnosed by the local doctor. It was a moot point as to whether the doctor was taken in by these rascals who hated school, and obviously wished to delay the inevitable confrontation with the teacher but I doubt whether any marks for artistic flair were given out when she saw the gummy mix of flags and heather in the crumpled box.

The Happy Harvest Days

In the Northern Highlands, summer days are longer but the weeks of growing season begin later and end earlier. There is one harvest, then the stubble fields, after being burned where required, would quickly produce some new sweet grass before the first of the autumn frosts nipped the air. Thus, at the back end of the summer, anxious eyes would scan the skies and heads would cock to sniff the air.

"Is there a bit of rain to come, Tommy?" John Wiseman would ask, and Tommy McSkimmin, from his diminutive height, squinting up through the smoke from his short pipe, and speaking past it's stem would give his best guess.

"Mmmyuss John, it might."

The bracken would begin to turn a little in places from drab green to yellow and the fields of golden corn, dotted with the blue of cornflowers and the crimson of poppies would sway in the breeze, remaining somewhat green in the more shadowy corners. John would walk around, here and there pulling a sample from a head and rubbing it through his fingers, then we would get a few dry days and out would come the binder to be pulled by the old Fordson tractor. There was no power takeoff and no hydraulic power, but the heavy knobbled iron wheels of the binder powered the complete system of cutting, gathering on the rotating belts, and the tying with twine.

This heralded great excitement in me as I would assist with lifting the lines of corn sheaves and 'stook' them, propping them up, heads firmly enmeshed in line in groups of eight, just like the sharp roofs of houses in order that the wind could get through them and encourage the ripening process whilst running off the rain.

In short trousers this soon became uncomfortable—especially if the stalks were a bit damp as our knees were used to spread the bottom half of the sheaves apart whist the tops were jammed together—and the lower parts of my thighs would became red with abrasion at the day's end.

There was also the quickly-learned skill of making a tying band out of spare stalks in order to gather any sheaves not properly bound. Twist the stalks into a quick rope, encircle the sheaf, twist it around itself until the sheaf was firm then tuck it under itself and the job was done.

I had also been taught by my father how to twist and form a tie-band out of green wands cut from hazel bushes or brambles, but that is another matter.

So the morning would pass and the dew would lift from the understorey grass, allowing my feet to dry, and at noon the kindly Mrs. Wiseman would appear with the magic basket.

Moist sandwiches, fresh scones and those little round pancakes, milk fresh from the cow the evening before. A veritable feast for a hungry young belly, then before we all got stiff, the afternoon's work would begin and we would toil on until the late afternoon sun turned into the soft glow of evening and it was time to stop, tidy the field and the machinery and go home for dinner.

It was grand to bask in the glow of approval from the old men, and their praise was genuine.

One year before I left school, for some reason John relinquished his protective hold of his tractor and binder and told Tommy to work it around the field whilst he dealt with some other jobs along the edges.

Tommy had taken part in the harvesting for many years and knew what to do, and the old tractor worked on one pedal which was located on the left hand footplate. It simply stopped the tractor and disengaged the clutch whilst the gears were changed with a noisy grating when the gear oil was cold.

It's a truth that witnessing an act and actually undertaking it are two different things, and somehow poor old Tommy panicked when the time came to turn at the end of the field. He lost the plot and along with it his nerve and forgot about the brake pedal. He ploughed straight over the low drystone wall separating the field from the hazel bushes on the river bank and the binder ended up sitting atop the ruined wall whilst the tractor engine stalled.

"Oh Tommy! Tommy!" cried John.

"Mmm-yuss, sorry John." The tractor and binder were extricated with some difficulty after we removed by hand the remains of the wall which had jumbled-up underneath the machinery, and luckily only minor repairs had to be carried out, the cutter having missed the stones.

After the stooks had stood for some days and they were well-dried, the tractor and trailer were used to cart the sheaves home where they were carefully stacked until the arrival of the threshing contractor. If I was lucky, the gathering would be done on a weekend when I could proudly stand in the trailer and pack the sheaves according to instructions.

The threshing was one of the more exciting events in the year and new John Deere or Nuffield tractors would arrive towing the thresher, then the tractor would be carefully positioned in order that the belt driven by the pulley would power the machinery and not fly off. These tractors were known about by the keen farmers' sons but had not yet arrived in the glens at that time. The corn stacks diminished in size until finally the ground level was reached, then the terriers and collie dogs would forget their usual squabbles and have a busy time dealing with darting rats.

So the day would pass with the hum of engines and the clank of machinery; the thrum of the wide belts and the click as the toothed joints encountered the metal drive wheels. This was added-to by the calls of the men above the din and the barking of the dogs with boys being occasionally remonstrated-to by watchful elders.

Big bags of corn were carried into the barn as the day progressed and the straw stacked ready for winter bedding.

Then silence. A day's clearing-up and eyes would then turn to the potato crop and another reason for boys and girls to stay off school and help with the nation's harvest.

The 'tattie picking' was a dirty and laborious task. Backs bent all day over long lines of earth and potatoes which had been rotated free of the raised drills, grubbing and placing the potatoes into wire mesh baskets, then carrying the baskets to sacks wherein they were emptied.

A keen eye in the form of the farmer would circulate after he had finished turning the drill and he would instantly spot the least hint of anything missed. Leaving the tiny ones in the field was frowned-upon as this would grow into a plant during the next year and interfere with future crops.

The wage was half a crown a day, which was one-eighth of a pound. About twelve and a half pence to you. Of course the worth of a pound was much much more at that time. The children were issued by the school authorities with an olive green card upon which the farmer had to mark each day worked and sign his name in order to certify that we had indeed attended the harvest work and not played truant.

Days at the Walking

I have mentioned elsewhere that walking was our main method of getting about, but it was also done for interest and pleasure when we had the time. Legs which were unthinkingly used for travelling miles every day were fit and toned, so walking for interest was done automatically and without much tiredness.

In this way the immediate territory around our houses was intimately logged whilst places much further afield were viewed with offhanded certainty as reachable if we had the time.

Thus it was with anticipation that I was told one Saturday morning by my father to get my jacket on and "come for a walk".

This was the August of my thirteenth year. Dad had his 'piece' bag on his back with the handle of his handbill sticking out of it (in case) and off we set.

First was the walk up through the remainder of the glen to the old graveyard at the head of Corriemony—which was a pleasant six miles in the fresh morning. My clothing was an old tweed jacket, cotton jersey over a cotton shirt (my only top), short grey flannel trousers, cotton socks and plimsoles and as this was my usual summer apparel I thought nothing of it.

The next stage was to mount the hill up the path out of Corriemony until it petered out, then carry on over the hill to Loch ma Stack.

This was another six miles, and inside the old deserted keep which had been erected on a little peninsula sticking out into the loch, Dad produced a can under which he lit a small fire of dry heather in order to brew some black tea with sugar in it.

The tea washed down a piece of bread and cheese, then some oatmeal and salt which was moistened into a thick paste and turned into a form of brose which I was ordered to "get it down you", along with the remainder of the tea.

The brose continued to work and swell in my belly, giving warmth and energy.

It was during one of these forays that we came across the whole forequarters—including heads—of two young stags which had been shot and the hindquarters taken away. I was curiously unmoved by the blood and intestines, but appalled by the wanton waste of two lovely creatures. To me, such animals were potential food, but I hated what I saw that day and it left a lasting impression.

The next stage, after an eyebrow-raised challenge (which inferred weakness) from my father about whether I wanted to turn back, was to continue over the hill and descend into Glenmoriston where we gained the road. This was another six miles. We walked down Glenmoriston, past the old shinty field—which is now a caravan site screened from the road by conifers—then walked along Loch Ness side for several miles until the hard road became quite uncomfortable through my plimsoles, there my father decided to halt until the next bus to Inverness arrived and we rode to the Drumnadrochit bridge.

It was another mere five miles up the road to our little cottage but after some twenty-three miles I was a bit tired and ready for my dinner.

I slept well that night.

A Lesson Perhaps

Only a Little Prayer

Whilst the flowers bloom
and little insects go their way
life goes on, the only time of now.
Deep is the scar on my soul,
and tightened lips, like fingers
groping to hold closed the wound,
bite back the salt in my mouth
and the hot tears that wash away
the pain in this my mind.
God give me the strength
to find a way to manhood
and stand firm in my resolve.

"Always put yourself last boy. There will be enough left at the back of the queue, and if not, there will be another time." These were the words of my father. The paradox lay in that while I was taught to observe the strict requirements of good manners and place myself last, other children who put themselves forward were readily accepted by those in authority who did not appear to recognise the diffidence exhibited by others, or have the depth of mind to deliberately bring out these quieter children in order that they might shine.

When I was seven and not long after I entered my second primary school I encountered a young spinster teacher who was something of a religious fanatic and who spent some considerable time with us each morning on religious studies. I had never before been introduced to the catechism and in my untutored ignorance I could not relate it to the forgiveness and love which were said to be in the Bible. The pamphlet did not make any sense to me, and frankly I found the strictures and implied threats in the wording more than a little disturbing. It was the stuff of nightmares to a young mind.

It was not long before the young woman lost all patience with me because I was new to the school and for some reason I could not memorise the words by rote. As a result I was left with weals on my wrists and arms from the leather taws which was a common method used by some teachers in order to instil their will in those days.

It was unfortunate that the authority of wielding the strap was frequently abused by those more inclined to the pleasure of its use, and not all so-called teachers came to the job as a paid vocation, but rather as a poor second best because they had failed in other academic avenues.

My father noticed these weals during the following weekend and demanded to know what was going on, so as we were incomers to the closed society of the glen and wishing to avoid the possibility of being accused of bullying a maiden teacher, he simply sent a letter to the school stating that from then on I should be regarded as a Roman Catholic and that I would not receive further Protestant religious instruction.

The irony was that now the physical bullying from the teacher ceased and I sat at the rear of the class, but she made sure that the rest of the children knew the contents of the letter. I was suddenly 'different' and as a result the rest of the children practically ostracised me because Roman Catholicism was very much disliked in the glen in those days.

Time seems to last forever during childhood, and I just could not understand why these people were blind to the fact that I, and others like me, were habitually bypassed in favour of a certain few. Where was this divine justice which I had been taught about, this equal sharing monitored by proper grown-ups who were of course, because of the respect instilled in us by our parents for adults, supposed to be endowed with wisdom and fairness?

I was unaware at this time that not all people had been taught to pay anything but lip service to justice and fair play, and I became naturally aggrieved, for despite striving both physically and mentally for approval—with the result that I won school prizes and was admitted into the Glenurquhart school shinty team—I somehow felt that I, and others like me, were tolerated because we were useful, but never really accepted.

It was for this reason that I left the Boy's Brigade only a few weeks after I begged my mother for the two shillings and sixpence with which to purchase a second-hand belt and cap in order that I might join and become 'one of the lads'. I eagerly trotted the five miles down to 'The Drum' community hall as the village of Drumnadrochit was termed, but my expectant pleasure was quickly quashed. It was immediately demonstrated that the squad into which I was placed was to be continually penalised by the middle-aged 'captain' who was a church elder because I was unable through lack of transport to attend the chapel over the hill at Cannich in Strathglass which was twelve miles away. For this reason marks were deducted from my squad every week and they never had a chance of winning any awards.

From my usual objective distance I saw that this hopeless situation would never be resolved. I felt a burden of guilt when I arrived at the village hall for our weekly evening meetings, and I knew that I would never be able to raise the money in order to attend their camps or courses, thus the situation became intolerable because instead of forming some form of comradeship I was creating hostility amongst my peers. After several such evenings I removed my cap and belt, said a polite goodbye and walked into the evening darkness. It was a lonely five miles back home.

It was during these years that I and some others were subject to the vindictive temper of another young female schoolteacher. She was a fervent follower of the American evangelist, Billy Graham and this young woman ran a small 'club' of pupils who joined her Scripture Union and were able to pay the subscription for the pamphlet every Monday morning.

Her 'disciples' were blessed with a beatific smile and warm words, whilst on the other hand those who would not dare to ask at home for the subscription and those who were of a different religious persuasion encountered a basilisk countenance whilst she belted the living daylights out of us at the least excuse. I heard later on in life that she had been kicked out of teaching because of her cruelty, but this was much too late for the children whose lives she had turned into a misery.

Her last bite at me was during the final examinations before I left school. Of all the pupils in the mixed-gender class, those destined to move on to college and university and others like me who were to become the world's labourers, I had gained one hundred percent in my maths and arithmetic papers.

On the following day when the results were handed out I found that despite my efforts she had deducted two points because in her opinion the handwriting in my workings-out in the margin whilst perfectly legible was not good enough.

I looked at her, shook my head with derision and went my way to my new beginnings. She was but a small soul after all but had been capable of great damage to youngsters, and herein lies the message that bitterness is easily gained under such circumstances, but it is best dealt with and left behind or it will mar one's life.

Perhaps the situation was not quite as I thought, but it is difficult for a child to see past the hope of innocent discovery and comprehend the unhappy complexity of religious differences which adults, for some reason have created for themselves. To suddenly encounter such implacable dogma within those who can be so otherwise kindly is startling and not a little frightening, so, for a child, one of the first negative aspects of mankind is stumbled upon and life begins to lose the vibrant hues of innocent spiritual love. The only place of safety and equilibrium I recognised remained amongst the quiet places.

During my latter years when dealing with children, I was very aware of this 'baggage' which had followed me with some sadness from my childhood, and whilst pandering to a degree to the undoubted abilities exhibited by most of the more precocious children, I made a point of encouraging the quieter ones forward in order to display their prowess as well.

It has always been a delight to me to watch their faces light up with pleasure when I called their names and praised their input, and I hope that it also made the others aware that quieter people have opinions and input of equal value.

Perhaps, in this way, I had been prepared at a young age in order that I might understand better, and maybe this was one of life's lessons for me. It certainly made me feel happy, but I hope not in a selfish way.

Slow-worms and Adders

I cannot tell for sure where or when I saw my first snake. I recollect, as a five-year-old running with other infants in some sort of breathless tension along a forestry track which was carpeted with brown, fallen spruce needles. One of the children had shouted "there's a serpent", and it was the signal for everyone to rush madly towards school. The dimly-lit forest track, bordered by tall Norway fir and Sitka spruce, was the most sheltered and direct route from home, and of course there was no serpent about in such an environment, especially at that time of day before the sun had time to warm the open spaces.

We knew that there was no serpent, but children love to be scared in a controlled way, and like the gregarious animals we were, we recognised safety in numbers.

There is a sort of horror and mystique connected with these creatures. Their very ancientness, perceived biblical connotations, and means of locomotion, serves to alienate them from human acceptance and as a result they slot well into the role created for them in human imagination as the evil counterpart of good in the Garden of Eden. It must be admitted that no one likes the idea of being inflicted with a venomous bite by a legless creature which of necessity slides along the ground, but then, we humans are so out of touch with matters natural, that it has been overlooked that adders, our only real venomous snake in these isles, will hiss in warning and get out of the way unless inadvertently trodden upon. I should imagine that given the strength and opportunity, any animal will naturally react in a defensive manner to a weight comparable to something like an elephant treading upon a human.

Having largely emerged from the age of superstition and nonsensical beliefs regarding these creatures which depend upon the sun for warmth, humankind quickly slipped from that phase into the other of mass denaturalisation of their own species. It is therefore by default that the only advantage to these animals in a habitat which is being rapidly destroyed, is that through indifference and ignorance in town outer limits, the remaining creatures are to a degree being left to their own devices.

Weather patterns of late are hardly conducive to the well-being of cold-blooded reptiles in Britain, and it is unfortunate that occasionally one still hears about a meeting with a wicked serpent where some human has dispatched the innocent beast because of superstitious fear and ignorance. In the old days there were tales of horrible deaths of children who had fallen foul of a nest of adders, and there are undoubtedly still incidents where people are bitten and rendered quite ill, or if they have an illness perhaps even die, because of the venom from these snakes. It must be remembered, however, that such occurrences are accidental and not by design. Adders do not seek the company of humans for any reason but only wish to be left in peace, and as far as I know, very few people even see these vipers on an annual basis, far less get bitten by them. There is a far greater chance of being hit by a motor car which has, through carelessness on the part of the driver, been turned into an instrument of destruction, yet we do not roam through the streets bashing motor vehicles or drivers to death in case one of them might cause the demise of a human.

One of my early experiences with members of the reptile family caused no little concern at home one summer evening. There were many mossy mounds underlaid by sand near the Sheneval burn close to the head of Glenurquhart where the forestry houses were situated, and these mounds were the favourite homes of slow-worms, those inoffensive members of the lizard group which for some reason had also lost their legs through the passage of time.

We children were fascinated by these glossy dark brown shapes with blunt tails, lying intertwined on the mossy mounds sleepily sunning themselves, and it was the normal thing to pick them up for curiosities sake. I was aware that some of our female family members would have had convulsions if they had known what we were up to, and I suppose that that was the beginning of recognition that girls were often given to different approaches to a subject.

So there we were—it was late afternoon after a hot day and I had a few of these creatures lazily wriggling amongst my shirt and vest when the hail came from the houses for the children to return home. I was probably about five-and-a-half at that time, and off I went, obedient to the call to be stripped and washed ready for bed.

Yowls of fright rang through the house as my mother and adult half-sister discovered these innocuous beasties inhabiting my nether garments, and I was chased from the house to get rid of the offending items. I took the poor creatures back to their moss-covered sand castle and watched them disappear down the burrows, then returned home to a sound ticking off and worried talk about picking up the wrong snakes. Such caution was justified as a mistake could cause great tragedy, but even at that age I recognised what slow-worms were.

Although I cannot remember exactly where I saw my first adder, I do recall an instant recognition of extreme caution. There was a feeling of capability which emanated from this creature, and I had a knowledge that I should keep well clear. This was a different proposition from the sleepy little slow-worms—this was a large, golden, well-marked hunter. Later to be recognised as a female.

A Growing Philosophy

A long number of years were to pass before I realised that out of my sum of experiences a philosophy of existence was forming. My somewhat solitary and disciplined youth, combined with a reluctance to intrude in already gathered company, resulted in a sometimes lonely existence, but I believe, however, that an inherited gift of objective observation was not soiled by cynicism, although my often rapid assessments of ostensibly charming people were sometimes misconstrued by those who had vested interests in believing otherwise.

My main stumbling block lay in a strong and often naïvely misplaced sense of idealism, but this might be balanced to a degree with a Cromwellian talent for self-examination which ensured in later years that I came to terms with, not what life had done to me, but what circumstances had caused me to unwittingly do with life. It was this growing recognition which came to form the basis of remarkable friendships in later years as things began to take on more meaning. I have no wish to aggrandise my existence in any way, as I slip into the traps of life all too often, but while my beliefs embrace the basic ideals incorporated in the various religions of the world, they, as a result, must remain free of career-motivated intrigue, pomp and ceremony. It has become evident that this philosophy, if one might call it such, is more prevalent and widespread than some might think, and my somewhat solitary recognition, and 'sorting out of priorities' helped render life acceptable as a testing ground for self-improvement, whilst moulding my outlook in order that I might become in some cases, a trusted friend of those whom I hold in high regard.

I was on several occasions urged by my father to beware of three things. The first was of nationalist flag-wavers; the second was to beware of politics; and the third was to hold in extreme reserve those who professed too much religion. I believe that he had good reason for all of those observations, and it can be no accident that all three have probably been the cause of as much evil, sustained corruption, and wars as anything else put together. The regular recurrence of the shoddier traits of human behaviour which constantly emerge from the self-appointed ranks of those who profess to be messengers of the universal God, can only serve to reveal how far removed from the original truth these mortals and the institutions which nurture them have strayed. Religions have split, fragmented, warred and tortured by reason of politics, feudal power, ambition, greed and superstition, and a percentage of what we are left with today is a filtration of brutally censored dogma calculated to play on the fears of mortals in order to keep them at heel.

It is as well to remember the basic truth that history belongs to the victor, and how many warring sides have clashed in the firm belief that God was in their camp? I adhere to no church; neither do I sit in judgement. I have, however, observed that many people have either deliberately ignored, or have been led by material lassitude to become unaware of that essential spiritual part of themselves which is important to common well-being. Condemned as a heretic out of my own mouth I might be by those who preach orthodox religions, but I would rather meditate as I wander in the unsullied corner of a lonely part of the hill and lay myself bare to the power of my maker. Therein lies the simple truth and if it is deemed so—then I'll pay my debts.

The South Side of Loch Ness

On an impulse, probably encouraged by the womenfolk of the house who always hoped for the magical pot of gold, my father and my eldest half-sister's husband decided to leave Glenurquhart for a short while and take up an offer of a contract to fell deciduous trees on the face of the hill overlooking the south bank of Loch Ness.

I recall now—after some memory-searching in the wee small hours—that I was about thirteen at the time. We had returned to Glenurquhart from Loch Broom to live in a farm building at Polmaillie and had been rejoined by my oldest half sister and her family.

It was during the late afternoon that we arrived with our bits of furniture which had been carefully loaded into the scrubbed cattle float, and before nightfall we were in residence in the two wooden huts on the bank of the loch below the old track.

Without more ado the men went up into the woods every morning, felling and clearing birch, alder and oaks in order to prepare the way for the planting of conifers by the Forestry Commission, so being the eldest child I accompanied them in order to assist, as there was no school, besides which I was useful and it was better to keep me occupied.

After a couple of months of this the son-in-law and my half-sister decided to leave as the life was too hard for them and they went off down with their children to live in the Lothian area.

We were alone, but my father had never backed away from a gentleman's handshake promise in his life and he was not about to begin now by walking out on the job, so he carried on alone, but I was on hand to help chop and saw the branches from the trees or pull on the other end of the cross-cut saw when a larger tree was to be felled.

Whilst my father was swinging his axe (he had a pair of them which had been forged for felling big hardwoods in the south), I levered the bare limbs together by using a trimmed sapling so that they were in-line and with the butt ends pointing downhill. I then fed the drag chain around the butt ends of the poles and attached it to the centre of the swingletree which was a stout piece of oak timber with iron loops on either end and an iron eye in the middle. The swingletree hung on the ground well clear of the pony's 'heels' and this was fastened by means of the loops to hooks on chains on either side of the pony which led through harness guides up to the collar.

I then led the pony downhill until we reached the road where I undid the drag and stacked the poles as neatly as possible, then trekked wearily back uphill with the mare again.

The reality was that once given the word to move, the mare took off at a trot and I had the dickens of a job keeping control and pace with her as she had found it much easier to pull the drag if she gained and maintained momentum. She weighed something like twelve hundredweight to my relatively puny frame so I depended a lot on her tolerance and patience.

So, every morning I raised myself, ran down to the loch in order to dip my head in the cold water, then went into the hut and had a breakfast of porridge or brose. I then took my 'piece' which consisted of a wide, thick soda pancake freshly made on the pot-bellied stove. Half of it was made into a cheese sandwich and the other half with jam, then that and a glass lemonade bottle filled with black tea was thrust into my bag and off we went to harness the mare and walk uphill. The tools were then sharpened and the day began.

My lessons in felling and clearing were progressing. I had callouses on my hands and I was as stringy as an eel, whilst constant practise at swinging an axe and billhook, and using the handsaws developed accuracy of hand and eye. Being allowed to use the sharpening stone was a gesture of trust, because in the first place a good edge could be ruined by bad use of the stone, and in the second, a slip of concentration and hand was heralded by a sharp sting and flow of blood. Thus I quickly learned to respect the working edges of tools as a properly sharpened axe, billhook or saw made life so much easier and were in fact much safer to use.

There is a time when familiarity does breed contempt and it caught up with me one day. I got the mare ready as usual and began the long haul downhill. As we worked on felling the trees we gained height, so the drag took longer as the weeks passed, and the weeks consisted of full seven days.

The mare was trotting downhill as usual, keen to get to the bottom of the hill for a breather, when about halfway down and in a dip which partly concealed me from above the drag of poles slithered a bit off-line from the path we had worn with previous dragging between the felled tree stumps. This was due to a crooked trunk which had worked underneath and as a result the drag hit a stump on one of the 'S' bends and lifted into the air at speed, rotating along its length and heading in my direction.

I instinctively leaped and landed on my backside with an uncomfortable thump with the rattling drag now sledging back onto the proper drag-path, but underneath me. I was in trouble as my ankles were already mixed up amongst the poles due to the weight of my landing and they had immediately begun working down through. If my feet reached the ground my ankles would be snapped and I was terrified that the drag might hit another such stump and roll over again whilst I was trapped.

Desperation took over from shaking fear. I leaned back and using my belly and thigh muscles, gradually pulled my lower legs upwards and free, then took the only chance I had on the rattling platform, I gathered myself to clumsily leap to the side.

The mare carried on downhill at a trot to the old road and I limped, shaking like a leaf, wiping tears of hurt and shame from my eyes and feeling very sick, to where the mare had stopped. I removed the drag, gave the old girl an extra 'blow' (which was the term for having a rest to catch up on our breath), and bathed both bruises and bleeding scratches with moss in a nearby ditch. The cold compresses of soaking sphagnum moss were very soothing.

When I got back up the hill it was remarked that I had taken my time, but I didn't tell my father about the incident as he might have been annoyed that I had been so 'slack'.

A couple of weeks later the contract came to an end and we moved back to the Glen where I had yet another period of adjustment. I hated returning to school and being treated like a child again, but it had to be.

The Highland Warpipe – My Army Years

That strange musical instrument was to become a powerful factor in my future life, because twenty-three years after I was introduced to the practise chanter, I realised my father's ambition. I obtained my Pipe Major's certificate at Edinburgh Castle. As a boy I had regularly practised on the chanter in the evenings—sometimes under duress as is the case of youngsters who are inside on a summer evening whilst they hear the rattle of home-assembled bicycles and chattering voices of their school companions—but practise I did, and during my early teens I was no stranger to being entered for competitions in Inverness.

Competitions and I did not mix well, but I did as I was told and in the true British way, failed to win prizes in a sportsmanlike manner. To be honest, I wondered what on earth all the fuss was about. For me, music was an art emanating from the soul to be enjoyed, not to be used as an egotistical club against one's fellow men, although I did thrill to the rallying sound of the pipes and fully understood how men would follow them into battle. Some people were better natural musicians than others, and there were those who were more dedicated in a single-minded way, but I was never like that.

When I experienced regret for not winning a prize, it was on behalf of my parents and not for myself. There was a musically gurgling river to fish out there and for me it had more substance than any single-minded striving to beat the other fellow.

Whilst I was still in secondary school and approaching the age of fifteen, I took my father's advice that there was little in the way of a future for me in the Glen, so I journeyed to Inverness and underwent the various physical and mental examinations required to join the army.

Having successfully passed the tests, I was then asked which was the regiment of my choice, and what I would like to train for.

I asked that I be trained as a piper in the Seaforth Highlanders, and was somewhat mystified and not a little suspicious that the recruiting sergeant wrote Drummer, and in brackets (wishes to be a piper), but it was then explained to me that there was no official position of Piper in the army as only Scottish, and affiliated regiments, have them, but that drummers were recognised as a part of any regimental strength, so I would go in as a drummer to be trained as a piper.

On the matter of joining as a Seaforth, I was assured that there were no vacancies at the time, but that there was a position for a boy piper in the Cameron Highlanders and that all the Highland Brigade Boys were in Fort George in any case, so I said "Fine", signed the dotted line for twelve years and three in the reserve, and the papers were then sent to my father to sign and finalise.

The fact that the recruiting sergeant was a Cameron Highlander, and a stranger to the truth on the matter of Seaforth vacancies was of little consequence, as both of those fine regiments amalgamated one year later in 1961, and we all became Queen's Own Highlanders.

In due course I presented myself to the guard inside the portcullis gateway of Fort George early in 1961, and entered into another world where life was regulated by bugle and bagpipe calls. Orders were obeyed first and questioned afterwards (if you dared), and you either toed the line, or endured stringent punishment parades—or jail.

It was as simple as that, and after a period of adapting, the life suited me very well. I was already hard and agile, amenable to discipline, and had unwittingly been trained to achieving over a hundred percent in everything I did (except for school attendance, although I somehow managed to make up time and win academic prizes in most years). So, cross country running, climbing, and field training were quite easy, whilst keeping myself and my kit clean was second nature due to the training I had received from my mother, both intentionally and inadvertently.

I also came under the direct control of a man who was to become a profound influence in my young life, and who, to my shame, I might have taken just a bit for granted owing to his unassuming manner, the ease by which he ran his unit and the way in which he passed on his skill. His title and name was Pipe Major Donald MacLeod, and at that time he was among the foremost pipers in the world. He was one of the senior army Pipe Majors at that time, and was serving his last few years in instructing the future Highland Brigade pipers.

As he was world famous in competitive piping, a number of us trainees would spend long periods of our free time simply absorbing his playing, and because I already had a little experience of junior competitive playing before I joined the army, it was not long before I was included in the more advanced group and being taken in hand by the man himself. He was aided by a number of extremely able staff members who came and went as time passed, and I met and got to know a number of the more eminent pipers of the day, whilst being sent on a senior pipers course to Edinburgh Castle where Pipe Major John MacLellan was in charge of Army Piping at the time.

So life flew by as I raced and ran, climbed and circumnavigated mountains with large loads on my back, danced across swords and played the pipes, all in competitive mode, and won a few bits and pieces whilst I gained the rank of Junior Sergeant and the inner 'me' emerged.

In the meantime a physical part of the inner 'me' was surgically removed when I curled up with peritonitis, but the gymnasium soon fixed that, then 1963 arrived, and it was time for a change.

Man's service training came to pass. I was assigned to an intake squad, and moved across the square to the training block. Off came my three stripes, the threads were removed and the uniform jacket pressed again. Sixteen weeks of intensive training were under way. I was back in the mode of obeying orders instead of dishing them out. But it hurt not a bit as I knew that what lay behind was a preparation for my future with the regiment.

Because of my experience, I was placed in nominal charge of two barrack rooms which housed eight men including myself, and we all raced through a period of extreme activity. It was certainly busy enough for me, but goodness knows how hard it was on those who had just joined up. That eventually came to an end and we all shipped out to join our various regiments leaving behind a double row of highly polished, but silent rooms, redolent with the smell of boot polish, brasso and blanco.

In the meantime I had spent the festive season in Gloucestershire in the company of one of the other squad members and it was there that I met his sister who was only sixteen at the time. Time was to pass and water flowed under the bridge, but it was that girl whom I again met and married several years later.

But back to the end of training. The RAF jet rumbled across the airstrip and off we went with a thump as the wheels came up, then many hours passed until we came back down to a blindingly sunlit airstrip where it seemed nothing existed except for throat choking heat and oil drums being heaved about by half naked servicemen who were burned brown as nuts.

We had landed in Aden.

It was just splendid to once again enter that cool airplane and get up into the air after refuelling, and this time it was late afternoon when we landed in a vastly different environment.

Banana palms and other strange greenery flashed past the wings as we landed at Anduki airport in Singapore, and my first sensation was of the hot humidity and the smells of all sorts of vegetation, some of it rotting, but not unpleasantly so.

Another phase of my life had begun. I was met by the duty driver who made short work of getting me to Selarang barracks which was not far from the notorious Changi prison, and my spell of acclimatisation began, but not before I was taken to the QM's stores and issued with my replacement jungle green clothing and equipment. My standard uniform for the next couple of weeks was to be the Tam o'Shanter bonnet, or TOS as it was known in the Scottish regiments, PT shorts, issue socks and boots, with the socks rolled down neatly over the tops.

The ironic 'Jock's' version was PT shorts and socks with boots rolled down.

Selarang barracks was built on an ex-Japanese prisoner-of-war camp, and I was told that the large sunken rectangles which became visible from the top tiers of the accommodation blocks revealed where mass graves had been dug and into which many prisoners had been interred.

On the periphery of the camp was an area of grass on which palm trees grew, and this was dotted with pits which had been dug as man traps by the original occupants. These pits were, for the most part, well filled with sand in order to cover the sharpened bamboo stakes which lay deep below, but in some cases the sand had settled to a depth of about six feet, and these holes were checked each morning by the outgoing night-guard in order to ensure that no drunken revellers were ensconced within.

It was not unusual for those who recognised themselves to be among the 'drunk and disorderly' after a night on the town, to stop the taxi along the road and break into camp without having to come in by the guard house. Sometimes the dark played funny tricks on drunken direction, and there were times when the odd body, still breathing but the worse for wear, might be discovered folded up double, or upside down in one of the holes.

Hot and supposedly moist, I felt as though I had been dried out in an oven. I was continually thirsty for a few days, and the 'cold water' machine and cold shower certainly got my attention. It was on the morning of my first muster parade in Selarang barracks when I noted that the flies appeared to be busy on my waistline, but on examination after the parade I discovered that for the first time ever known to me I had been dripping sweat. I had, until then, apart from the most strenuous cross-country run, never sweated properly before.

The main body of the regiment was over on Brunei at the time, which is a part of the island of Borneo and I was to join them at the first opportunity after I had become more used to the heat.

Pye dogs, Chinese and Malays, Alsatian patrol dogs with blotches of blue medication dye, and their handlers, a young chinese cobbler with whom I became friendly, Tiger beer, curry, and that sun which refused to let up until six o'clock each evening when the heavens clouded and opened to deliver a deluge for fifteen minutes. It was a vastly different reality, and so too was the one I fell into on the evening when the taxi driver drew up too close to the monsoon ditch during one of those deluges, and I stepped straight into four feet of floating filth in a monsoon drain in the middle of Singapore!

The taxi driver drove away smartly before I could get back in and come to terms with his particular form of entertainment, but it was probably just as well as they had a very strong brotherhood which were long used to feuds.

In due course I was told to pack my kit, and I was taken to the airport where I was ushered into a Hastings light transport plane, and we took off, tail finally leaving the ground, for the island of Labwan.

Labwan was a more tropical version of Aden, in that there was hardly anything else in evidence apart from sweating servicemen rolling 45-gallon oil drums about. There was no ceremony, but I was helped to gather my gear, pointed to a jetty not too far away, and given the name of a motor-launch which, presumably, was run by the pioneer or supply corps.

Presenting myself to the sergeant who appeared to be in charge, I was told to get myself and my gear aboard the grey-painted launch of some thirty feet in length, and we slipped away into the late afternoon on a fairly quiet sea.

I remember the light fading and the phosphorescence on the bow wave with equally phosphorescent flying fishes skittering ahead, and in time the darker loom of the land indicated that we were arriving.

Another base camp, and another period of adjustment whilst the regiment returned from some task they were engaged in upcountry. I was taken by Land Rover to a row of quite comfortable bungalows on the outskirts of the town of Brunei where I was given a bunk and shown where to find a meal.

Five o'clock in the morning, and who needed a call at reveille! A devout gentleman wailed his devotions through a loudhailer from a tall minaret down in the town not far away, and the base-camp monkey came through the window to claim his morning attention and tidbits.

He was a selective little pest, and whenever he got out of hand and got berated, he would disappear screaming, to return with a larger human version who looked not unlike himself. This human was one of those incorrigibles of the British army. He never looked tidy, but was a most efficient driver, and most importantly, beloved guardian of the little monkey.

Another week or so passed, then yet another trip up country, this time to join 'Shining "A" company, No. 1' platoon, where I was to become their temporary piper and additional rifleman. My preferred weapon was the 7.62mm LMG which had taken over as a direct copy of the famed Bren gun, but the issue of the much lighter SLR rifle was preferable in such dripping heat. The regiment was bivouacked at the edge of the jungle, and I settled in—but not for long—No. 1' platoon was then shifted to a place called Lutong on the coast where we relieved another platoon on pirate patrol duties. The bagpipes were put into safe store.

So the time passed in night patrols where we specialised in fighting off sandflies, weapon training practise, volleyball and eating delicious meals off banana leaves cooked by the old Malay further along down the pathway. He was probably paid by the pirates to keep a watch on us in turn, but we'll never know.

Then came the call, and 'A' company regrouped to embark onto a number of large landing craft. These were large enough to carry tanks and trucks, and we were allocated places on the top plates of these rather ungainly vessels then each issued with a couple of cans of oxtail soup which, with the aid of a ring pull, were self-heating from a central core.

The day passed. Water bottles diminished in volume, the deck plates got very hot, we got par-boiled and it was better not to move and encounter hotter metal. The cans of soup were inedible and tasted solely of some noxious chemical heating compound, and were tossed overboard to poison the local fish, then came night, and it got cold in our sweaty jungle shirts, with the webbing digging into the more vulnerable and sweat-softened parts of our anatomies.

Whoever designed that particular style of webbing, and declared it suitable, should have been sent to hell with it all wrapped around his neck.

Dawn came, and we saw the jungle-clad banks appear ahead. We had arrived at the correct location of a creek mouth on the shores of Borneo, and from the gut-gurgling movement of the large landing craft, we lowered ourselves into the shallow hulls of dugout canoes.

This was more like it, and we paddled our way upstream until we were given the signal to land. There, in a clearing, we were briefed, and again set out for several hours along trails and across fallen tree bridges, stopping occasionally to take a drink and remove the friendly local bloodsuckers, until our scouts met us and we were deployed silently around a village.

This was the stuff of which every lad dreams about, but after standing at the alert for some time with my rifle cocked and at the ready with bayonet fixed, with the nearest field of vision scant yards away, I realised more than ever that if some stranger came into my field of view, he might not have a friendly look on his face—and that I might well have to do something about it.

Apart from a visit from 'the ramrod' who was my platoon sergeant, who did a tour using the pre-arranged signal in order to ensure that all was well, the village was taken quietly before the occupants and their 'visitors' could properly awake, and prisoners were taken along with a lot of propaganda literature. The raid had been a success, and with no blood spilled.

The return to base was a bit more expedient, and all too soon we were embarked onto the *HMS Albion,* a helicopter carrier which was to take us back to Singapore. Apart from a couple of about-turns when we were placed on standby in case we were going to be recalled, and a stop for refuelling with avgas, the return over a few days was quite uneventful.

Soon after our return to Singapore, the first joint annual 'open' day was held on the shooting ranges at Neesoon which was not far from the Gurkha Barracks. This event was to be known as 'The Cabar Feidh Shoot' and it was conceived as a few days of fun shooting competitions using our various weaponry, with the more serious side of discovering the shooting talent within the whole regiment, so officers, warrant officers, NCO's and squaddies alike were one and the same for the day; all being formed into teams and competing elements.

It was during this three-day stint that to my surprise I was elected into the Battalion 24 best shots, along with one of my old training squad peers, Murdo Macdonald, who was eventually to become a Quartermaster Major.

There was some fun and games during the days of this shooting. Some wag emptied the contents of a silver salver with a large cover and replaced it with a huge fruit spider which was a hand-span in width. One of the officers' ladies opened the salver and there was an almighty shriek with all hell letting loose, but the culprit was never found.

Another was when we had the run-down from three hundred yards to one hundred with the new GPMG machine gun which was built, like the rifle and light machine gun, around the calibre of 7.62 millimetre.

This gun was intended to replace the Light Machine Gun and the heavier old Vickers in platoon and support roles utilising light and heavy barrels and it was still very much in the field trial stage at that time. Teams of two per gun were timed to see who got the best score overall at the three ranges—sprinting with the unloaded gun in between.

One of the Company Sergeant Majors, 'Bones' as he was nicknamed, was a bit unfamiliar with the gun as very few of the regiment had handled one. He had absent-mindedly fidgeted with carrying handle catch whilst awaiting the next whistle to dash forward, and there was great hilarity when he was seen racing down the range with the barrel which he had inadvertently released from the gun.

So the years passed. Gwendy and I got married, then a year later our first daughter, Kathleen was born in the military hospital in Munster in Germany. I did my stuff with the regiment in the pipes and drums and running and shooting teams, and in the course of gaining rank, also gained my Pipe Major's certificate after a nine month course, once again in Edinburgh Castle.

En-route to the course I was temporarily stationed in Aberdeen at the Brig 'O Don barracks in Aberdeen where the boys' service was then stationed and I was placed on the training staff.

That time was a mix of interest and boredom. The interest lay in that I held evening classes in fishing, fly tying and rod building. I was able to fish on several nice waters outside Aberdeen and I made friends with a wolf at Hazelhead Park.

Our second daughter, Ruth, was born during our stay at Aberdeen, and I dismounted from duty in the early morning in order to cycle down through Aberdeen and visit with Gwendy and our new baby daughter.

On perhaps a more boastful note, I also jolted the senior staff of the non-musical branch of the boys service as a 'mere musician' by winning the sweepstake shootout with the GPMG at the end of our day's annual classification. We were each given 112 rounds of ammunition as the annual supply was required to be used-up and were timed in rapid bursts of fire. Within the time allowed of four minutes I put ninety eight out of the hundred and twelve bullets into the four inch bull at three hundred yards. It was a bit of a surprise to them but I had been qualified to wear my marksman's badge throughout my service years and I had retained my exacting fitness which ensured that I could match their best endeavours at any time.

The boredom bit was in trying to coax teenage lads to do their duty under a new regime of political correctness. I despise bullying and psychological manipulation. I also hate abuse of authority and rank, but in straight soldiering orders have to be obeyed or people are liable to get killed. The new order of things to come which I experienced during that brief interlude made me very uneasy and I was glad of my imminent posting to Edinburgh Castle in order to study for and pass my nine months pipe-major's course.

It was after this that I realised that for me routine soldiering had become a bore. I could see little future in awaiting my turn for further promotion which might or might not materialise, besides which, I now had a young family to rear, and I chose to do it in a more stable climate than that of a continually moving army camp. My twelve years were up, I had done my bit and I now felt free to pursue my own course. The army days were over and it was time to take my young family to a more settled environment.

Applecross

S o where did my life amongst nature begin? Was it during that
remote boyhood which seems to speed ever faster into the past as
the years advance, or was it really when I left the army and gained
work in the Highlands? So much had happened in the intervening years,
but for me the reality of my years amongst nature seemed more important
than those of my time in the army. I had enjoyed the comradeship and
in extending myself, and I also enjoyed the immediacy of decision and
enactment of that decision, but I realised that the army was changing and
I was becoming a dinosaur in my own time. My problem was that I was
torn two ways. The first was that I have always been beset by a strong sense
of duty and responsibility, but the other side revealed that I had never
become institutionalised so it was easy for me to move on rather than live
in a rut.

I had made the decision to raise our children in an environment much
like the one I had known as a boy, but when the hand of chance directed
me to seek employment on a Highland estate, I had no idea at that time
that I would end up in Applecross as I could hardly have chosen a more
isolated area; a peninsula which had, by and large, escaped the notice, and
therefore the doubtful 'benefits' of a steadily advancing world.

At that time, there were still numbers of deer in the corries of the
Beallach na Ba over which the main roadway traversed. This was the
only motorised route into Applecross in those days, and that in itself was
considered difficult enough as the road twisted its way around hairpin
bends from sea level to over two thousand feet over a distance of five miles,
with a similar descent on the other side. Motor traffic was still relatively
infrequent and the deer, especially the stag parcels, had not been forced to
find quieter corners. Estate transport was, for the most part, still rare and
my first set of wheels was a bicycle which I bought myself, but for which I
received an annual tax rebate of the princely sum of six pounds for repairs
per annum.

I was on leave from my regiment in Germany and my little family staying temporarily with my parents in Glenelg when a 'phone call from Neil MacPherson, the factor of the estate on which my father worked, informed me that if I was still interested in an estate job, there was a vacancy on Applecross Estate, and that I should get over there and take a look.

There was no form of public transport between Kyle of Lochalsh and Applecross at that time, and my own location at Glenelg made things difficult. I was told, however, that if I made my way to Kyle on a certain day, an Applecross fishing boat would take me over to Toscaig at the southern tip of the Applecross peninsula where I would be picked up.

There was nothing for it but to borrow my father's bicycle and pedal my way the thirty-odd miles, over Rattagan ridge to Glensheil and thence to Kyle. I then made my way down to the fishing boat pier and located the boat which was to ferry me into the future. She was named the *Catriona*, and the journey was made pleasant by the friendly enough curiosity of the crew whom I was to become more acquainted with in the years to come. But first I had to finish my term with the regiment in Germany, and break ties which had become strong through time. It was not until I made my final round of the various regimental departments with a clearance chittie which had to be signed by all, that I realised just how strong those bonds of comradeship had become. The die, however, was cast, and I walked out past the regimental standard at the front gate for the last time. That part of my life was put behind me, but occasional dreams of regimental duties, the bane of my life, were to remain with me for some years.

A Return to Country Life

The Hill is Quiet

In skies hazed blue before the eventide,
a star glow crests the ridge towards the sea.
Shadows stretch to fold with reaching hands,
and hollows blessed with warmth from morning sun
retreat in darkness, dusk comes to the land.

The hill is quiet as nature rests a while,
and sounds of creaking harness fill the void,
as patient ponies plod with nodding heads,
clinking their iron clad hooves on hidden stones,
as laden down with stags they homeward tread.

Leading in careful stride and searching glance,
a figure sets a pace and seeks a way
through heather knolls and bogs where dangers lie
towards that easy haven of the path.
The evening star grows brighter in the sky.

An anxious, thoughtful ghillie marks the route
to lead his pony on the safest ground.
His coaxing words of warning to the bay
of cracks, soft places, searching with a frown,
the darkening hollows set upon the way.

Black curves etched against the purpling sky,
show swaying antlers tied with creaking straps,
adorning heads that earlier scanned the slopes
in sunshine, basking high among the rocks,
before the shots which finished all their hopes.

And last the Rifle pacing on behind,
whose work is nearly over for the day.
Watching the saddle and its swaying load,
and thinking of his bath and blisters both;
his aching feet are looking for the road.

With sighs of gladness as they reach the path,
'tis several miles before that welcome glow
of cheerful windows' yellow bathing grass,
and noisy larder, knives and repartee;
perhaps the chink of bottle on a glass.

Then all is over, darkness closes in,
the hill is quiet, the goat birds rise to call,
a grouse gives voice as Reynard makes his play,
the killing time is done.
Two souls flit on their way.

On my return from Germany after completing twelve years in the army, I settled in to my new job at Applecross. As expected, I experienced a substantial drop in wages to that of an agricultural worker, but the die had been cast, and I had lived off the land before.

I had been married for seven years, and my wife, Gwendy, had delivered two of our three daughters into the world. The eldest, Kathleen, was due to begin school, and now was the time to put down roots and give them the essence, but hopefully not too many of the knocks, of my earlier life. There were the advantages of a more modern world, improved medicines and enlightened outlooks on most subjects, but I temporarily forgot that to enter a place like Applecross, at that time, was to step back almost thirty years.

There was little enough transport to be had, and certainly none of a public nature. There were no public services except for a three-man road squad with a Land Rover as their main vehicle, and a dustbin collection which was operated by the home farm, and disposed of on a local tip.

The doctor had no means of transport into the more remote places, other than to obtain a pillion ride on a motorbike, and agricultural wages had not improved in actual value since the Dark Ages. I did, however, own a twenty foot, cruiser stern launch which I had bought as a beach-buried derelict during my last army years, and which my father and I had resurrected. It was an excellent sea boat, and I caught regular supplies of whitefish and mackerel with handlines, often supplying the older folk in the village with fish they never seemed to need, but accepted nevertheless. That boat was an important tool for survival, as were our only other forms of personal transport, two bicycles.

Along with fish, we were able to make-do with my earnings and farm 'perks'. Gwendy, who was always marvellous at money management, adapted readily to taking down old woollens, and re-knitting them into jerseys and stockings. I was to berate myself privately in later years, but Gwendy, who was always a staunch supporter, pointed out that we had achieved exactly what we set out to do, and that was to give the children a stable and common sense environment in which to grow up.

Nevertheless, it disturbed me when I saw that other children were more indulged in material things and worldly privileges, as I knew that our girls could not avoid making comparisons, and must therefore feel somewhat deprived. According to personal experience, boys usually appear to shrug things off and make do, but little girls sometimes have tongues far sharper than their years, and nice things are important to most of them.

Our way of life, however, appeared to work out in the end, and those young women went out into the world to stretch their wings in the city of Edinburgh, and were never out of work. So much for country bumpkins, and so much for the 'street wise' city dwellers who can never find jobs.

We encouraged our daughters in working hard at their education, not in order to fulfil any ambitions of our own, or to reap any reflected glory for ourselves. This union was, apart from our feelings for one another, about creating a future for our children, based on decent social principles and a belief in divine justice, while rejecting materialism and selfishness.

We made it clear that the girls owed us nothing except our personal right to live with a certain amount of dignity amongst the local populace. If they decided that they loved and respected us, that was fine. On the other hand, I assured them that once they were up and out into the world, they could always depend upon us for support in a crisis, but we in turn owed them nothing, and would not be used as a crutch for idleness.

Having witnessed in the past the manipulation of spuriously asserted debts because of blood ties, I resolved never to inflict this crippling anchor on any of my family. They were never to live under the oppressive cloud of psychologically manipulative pressure, but were to be free to choose their path, and the manner in which they used their earnings. The girls had been given an allowance during their teenage years, and from this they were taught to cater for their annual clothing, savings and social life. They were also taught to bake and cook, sew and patch clothing, as well as grow vegetables and gather firewood.

In essence, they were far more useful with their hands than many of their male contemporaries, and that knowledge, once gained, was carried lightly.

I pointed out that, when the time came, they would inevitably do as they pleased regarding their choice of partners and way of life. It was, therefore, fair that Gwendy and I, the original partners, should be able to arrange some things to suit ourselves, as we would once again depend upon one another for company and solace once they had left.

I hoped that this would set a just foundation for their future lives as I abhor the dictum that children are in some way always in debt to their parents. After all, children never ask to be brought into the world, and it's the job of any mother or father to ensure that their offspring are made ready and able for their own adulthood. If respect and unstifled love blossom as a result, then that is a fulfilling bonus.

Our three girls, now all women, are our best and loyal friends, and I would like to think that we are also on the best of terms with their men.

But back to our entry into Applecross life.

I had joined the estate as a general estate worker, but just like the person who enlisted in the army as a drummer in order to become a piper, my job description was about to change, and this time without intent.

My civilian work began in the November of 1970, but the first three months came under pre-release training and demobilisation leave prior to being transferred to the army reserve. I was actually released from the regular army in February 1971, and this was done at Glencorse Barracks outside Edinburgh.

Later on that month, I was clearing and burning limbs and branches from a hardwood clearfell area, when I was visited for the first time by my new employer, Andrew Wills.

I liked what I saw when I shook hands with the man, although I realised almost right away that I would have to adjust my way of thinking in order to accommodate what I perceived as a measure of mild eccentricity. I had absolutely no qualms after the visit, but settled happily to get on with my work during the months to come. I had chosen a way of life in order to give our children a base from which to work, and as far as I could see, that was what parenthood was about.

A year of steady work passed, and one morning I was sent over the hill as a passenger in the estate lorry to be dropped off at the base of Corrie nan Arr in order to assist Donnie 'Russel' MacKenzie to spread bags of phosphate around a small plot of conifers.

The truck drove off and I stood amidst the silence, waiting for the next move, then I saw a man striding down across the knolls towards me. This was Donnie. We shook hands and his grin was as open as it was searching. Within the hour we were talking away as though we had never been apart and it is only now whilst I sit here that it has come to me that I was possibly sent over to him so that he could take a good look at me. We were to become very close in the years to come and it was quite common for us both to know exactly what the other was thinking—or at a distance know what the other was about to do. This must sound a bit odd, but we were both from backgrounds where the old senses were not obliterated and we both had experiences which could not be explained.

Since I myself have retired I was honoured to help carry Donnie to his last resting place, and say goodbye to yet another gentleman of nature from an iron generation. One of the two best shots in the wartime Lovat Scouts, sniper and behind-the-enemy-lines observer, he was my 'big brother' and mentor, and he never disappointed me.

The second February after I arrived in Applecross I was again approached by Andrew Wills who, in a round-about way, broached the subject of my job description by asking if I would like to go to Rhum.

I must confess to appearing a bit ignorant at this point, although I could hardly be expected to realise what he was on about, so I said, "I've just settled down here, why would I want to go to Rhum?"

He gave me an impatient look of the sort which was to become familiar over the next twenty-six years. Andrew was usually several mental steps ahead of the rest of any company, and just assumed that they were there with him—crystal ball as well. In this instance he said, "I meant, to attend the stalkers' course!"

I was a bit taken aback, and my impulse to inform him that I did not yet possess the mandatory crystal ball, never came forth. Probably because if I opened my mouth, it would have stayed open. As time passed, I learned to anticipate his thoughts, but it was quite amusing when we both leapt ahead at different tangents, both logical, but with totally opposite results.

Our protracted conversations on deer, their management and the things which made them 'tick' passed many a long hour as we walked in the hills, and from this talk a comfortable companionship evolved which we enjoyed for many years.

Our partings and meetings were done with a look and casual nod, and things just picked up where they had stopped. The only disconcerting thing was that, at times, he would mention something I had said before his departure, as though it was still fresh in my mind for further discussion, and I once told him that he did not have to work at being an eccentric as he was there already.

But I am jumping ahead of the narrative.

After a period of steady estate work, mainly in forestry duties, I had been let off the leash and told to accompany the stalkers on some maintenance duties. On one occasion I met Donnie 'Russel' MacKenzie on the Kishorn side of the estate in order to help him spread some rock phosphate in the Coire Nan Arr plantation, and on another to accompany both him and Donnie Cameron for a day at the hinds. I simply took these as just other working excursions, the latter being a real treat, but I was obviously being weighed-up by these men, whom I came to like and respect very much.

I was to become very close to Donnie 'Russel' during the years we worked together, and we were sometimes mistaken for father and son, or brothers. His examples of honesty, marksmanship and fieldcraft were exemplary, and his manner of transferring his skills was unconscious. I simply wanted to emulate his high standards.

I had no pretensions of becoming a member of the stalking team, as I subconsciously and without envy, placed their job beyond that of anything I would aspire to. I always felt extremely natural and comfortable in their company, but that was not to say that I had any ideas about being asked to join them. It was, therefore, a real shock to the system to try to absorb the implications of the invitation in a few seconds.

Somewhere at the back of my mind I suspected that there might be a huge learning curve ahead, but I swallowed my doubts and accepted the challenge, as usual. It took me about twenty seconds to look Andrew Wills in the eye and say, "Yes, thank you very much," and he gave that long, quiet considering look of his, nodded his head, and left.

Dan MacCowan, a native of Applecross, whose father and grandfather were both head gardeners on the estate, was home on holiday from his job—I think with the Nature Conservancy at the time—and Andrew arranged that as Dan was travelling to Rhum, he would give me a lift and see me to the other side off the ferry. The course was held during August, and I was thrown into the deep end of stalking after my return home.

I was lucky in the respect that all of the stalking was done for family and friends in those days, and I had plenty of time in which to familiarise myself with the hill.

I immediately liked Dan. He had a charming and open manner, and was completely relaxed and self-effacing despite his obvious intelligence and thorough knowledge of wildlife. Dan became a sound friend of our family through the years, and he will always remain so.

As I stated earlier, I was also to get to know Andrew Wills during our subsequent stalking forays, and ventures into various carpentry projects, and he remained exactly the same throughout the period I knew him. We were to become friends within the bounds of our working relationship, and it was well enough known by that time that I spoke my mind to both employer and workmates, whilst obliging the local people with help and civility whenever possible. There could be no ideas about toadying. I trod my own space, and fought my own corner when the occasion demanded. I also opened my mouth far too often for comfort.

I was probably one of the few stalkers of that period to speak without fear or favour in such a manner, and still retain my job, but I believe that Andrew had probably reached his own conclusions by the time it came for me to speak my mind, and I made sure—to the best of my ability—that he never had cause to regret it.

It was not bravado of any sort, but the way I was brought up. Of course I felt that I was putting my employment in jeopardy, and felt some apprehension for the future, but my father would have been disappointed if I had let myself down, and I would have despised myself.

As soon as I became immersed in the stalking side of the estate, it soon became clear that a form of strict deer management was in progress, but mainly within the bounds of that which was acceptable in the old tradition.

Donnie was a bit more progressive in his approach than the older stalkers, Willie and Donnie Cameron, but at that stage the results of selective culling, as it was still in its relative infancy, were not really appearing, and there was little proof for presentation, so there was naturally a quiet reservation on the part of the older stalkers and more vociferous opinions about the new ideas from some members of the landowner's family who liked things done the old way.

I was told by Donnie, that he and Donnie Cameron had been given rifles, and that they had cleared a lot of small, poor quality hinds off the place. It was, however, going to take at least another ten years before the work culminated in unmistakable improvements to both heads and bodily condition, and by that time I was treading even further down the road in 'new' management ideas, and without the constant worry of offending the sensibilities of the older men who were now retired.

In the meantime, Kenny Cameron, son of Willie and Katie, stepped from his annual role of assisting his father with the sheep and ghillieing at the stags, to full-time stalker in his father's place. I first met Kenny when he was twelve, and here he is now—nearly fifty.

In the old days, it was not unknown to stalk a particular stag on several consecutive occasions in order to secure him. The general dictum was that only 'proper' mature stags should be shot, and anything younger or under thirteen stone in weight was taboo. A few young hinds with no calves at foot, or older ones considered as yeld (not having calves), were shot for the pot and to be sent south by train to the employers.

By and large, the policy of shooting only mature stags is no bad policy as it ensures a variety of interesting heads to stalk, if one is not bothered about improving head quality and shape, but the new reasoning was that in order to create an overall improvement, all doubtful material should be removed, no matter what age or gender the beast. It was not considered suitable to have a 'bad' head or sub-standard hind and calf eating the meagre winter supply of valuable fodder.

I did, however, have reservations about shooting staggies before they had reached the age of demonstrating what they could do with their head shape and bodily condition. It was obvious that a poor little knobber with a ragged coat, obviously suffering during the hind season, had best come off, but after that period it was better to wait until they became young stags of at least three years old and were producing some market weight. A stag is usually showing what he is going to be made of by then, and that is the time to weed out the poorer specimens if you grudge further grazing.

With strict selective culling of both hinds and stags, it was proved—within two deer generations, or twenty years—that the forest could produce fine-looking hinds and calves, as well as heavy stags with good heads. From a top quality head of eight points in the 1960s, we progressed to heads of twelve plus points, with one seventeen pointer and a few imperials in the early 'eighties.

Further population experiments followed, and we reduced the herds even further in the late 'eighties. This produced an increase in body weights to what I believe to be optimum for a west Highland deer forest, but this evidence was still rubbished by some part time 'hobby stalkers' who had, what Rabbie Burns would call, "guid conceit o' themselves".

In all those years, the food quality remained the same. The hill was governed, apart from our several intended reductions, by a one-sixth selective cull of stags, and constant selective hind and calf culling. We never fed the deer, and several attempts to introduce them to mineral licks failed.

The deer did it on their own, with the help of disciplined rifle work in place of natural predation and a number culled according to an annual census. All it took was a lot of determination.

By this time I had been writing, firstly for the *Scottish Field* on a couple of occasions, then for the *Stalking Magazine* as a regular contributor for sixteen years. During this period I had a few clashes in the letters pages, but the positive side was that I was able to 'spread the word' and in the process, met and made some fine enduring friends. Donnie retired and I was invited to take the post of head stalker, then later, look after the estate woodlands and sawmill. Donnie's son Christopher joined me for a couple of years, and as he and Kenny Cameron, Willie Cameron's son, had been in school together, they were a bit of a brain-trying handful at times. Both were of course from several generations of stalking and shepherding and both were excellent shots and skilful with the telescope and at the stalking. It must have been difficult for these young bloods from generations of hill work to have an incoming overseer like me, but time has passed and the generosity of their breeding showed true. For a good number of years Christopher has been looking after the estate where his grandfather stalked during the era of the Second World War, and Kenny is still stalking the deer on Applecross and looking after his own flock of sheep, in the company of David Abraham who now holds the post I once occupied but on a somewhat-reduced deer forest.

Eilidh (Gaelic for Helen), our youngest daughter, had been born in Raigmore Hospital in Inverness in the meantime. There was no ambulance in those days and Gwendy went into early labour so she was shipped away, busily making out a shopping list and accompanied by the local nurse in the local grocery van. They had to drive over the Bealloch na Ba after the van had been cleared of its produce and an old mattress had been laid on the floor—just in case.

It was a long journey on single track roads in those days and Gwendy was in hospital for over a week so she had plenty of opportunities to make out fresh shopping lists.

A Chain of Lochans

The Awakening

Through leaves dark spangled
in this quiet slumbering world of gold hued dawning,
black boned branches of ancient pines
frame the still dark pool of fading stars,
and I, in the hissing stillness
watch the sun's vanguard steal over the eastern marches.

Then in a new awareness, a pink glow
softly treads a path o'er the deep cut loch,
crossing the waves of ancient seas
to the rocks on which I stand,
made of the same old dust as I.

And in the cold filtered light of a new day
I stand enfolded in the bosom of the universe
watching water, land and air,
and all the elements of physical being
used by the mystic flow of searching souls
on their journey to the sun.

The first time I ever set eyes on this hidden chain of small lochs I was alone.

I was struck by the feeling that I had come on a very secret place, and that I was completely alone at the beginning of the world. There was no road round the Applecross peninsula coast in those days, and a considerable walk over what was steadily becoming through lack of use and neglect, a rough coastal track, was involved in order to reach the sea-level base of the area I describe. Stalking this part of the deer forest was almost impossible because of the distances and terrain which our Highland ponies could safely cover in one day, and whenever we did look into this place during the stalking season, it was in effect looking over a boundary to a strange and largely unexplored land. The stalking had of necessity to be undertaken in the direction of home once we left the track, or above the three accessible routes into the hill known for ponies at that time. The furthest starting point we could sensibly use, required a six mile trek round the coast from Applecross before proper stalking activities into the hills began, and this often meant that the same six miles had to be repeated back home at the end of the day; sometimes in moonlight if Mother Nature was in a kind mood. To infer that this was untouched and virgin land would be tantamount to repetition of the arrogance shown by others in recorded history as I was very aware that this remote corner of the Highlands which I sat and contemplated, had at one time been busily peopled with folk who used it according to what nature could offer, both in what was taken and given to the land, and mostly with their bare hands.

Around the entrances to the lochans which were joined by short streams, patches of fresh green turf were formed as a result of nutrients being washed from one water system to another. As the water slowed at the loch entrance the sediments settled in the process, and fine level banks built up on which grew these short nutritious grasses. Near some of these entrances rested tumbled but recognisable shapes of moss-covered stone remnants of what had once been the walls of basic summer dwellings, but the time of these dwellings and those who used them was long gone. Now the secluded little world was devoid of voices, and a period of quiet, broken only by the sleepy gurgling of water, pervaded these isolated corners where wading birds fluttered and piped amongst the stones, and pipits, wrens, voles, and otters now held sway. Small trout swam in the little water worlds, patrolled by dragonflies and damselflies of iridescent red, green and blue, and each year thousands of frogs of all sizes congregated there. They made their living on the abundant fly life, whilst on the bottoms of nearby pools, newts rested with outstretched legs in shallow water, miniature dragons descended from a primeval age, and occasional foraging otters rummaged their way down the little streams, turning over the slimy black stones in search of eels.

It was evident that even the deer seldom used the area around the lochans except as crossing points from one resting place to another, and this now secret hollow in the hills, almost two miles in length and hidden from the seaboard by a heather and bed-rock ridge, had an air of mystery and waiting. As I sat watching, the dampness seeped from the moss-grown rock through my tweeds, but I was long used to such things, and the subconscious message of chill was ignored as it occurred to me that here was a simile of life. There was a beginning and an end. The beginning lay in several natural drains which gurgled and tumbled their way through the life experience of the hills to join at last, sowing the seed in the womb of the first lochan.

In this womb, a place where the waters joined, silts had settled to form a large reed bed where everything quieted and the water was cleaned. It then emerged at the other end as a small meandering burn where little trout darted from moving shadows. Each time the water met a hollow, it had settled again to form a large pool or lochan, and each of these lochans symbolised a period of life with short stretches of connecting river joining each experience. The first of these lochans is known as *Loch Dubh na H'oichde*, the *Black Loch of the Night*; and the genesis of this naming is as shrouded in mystery as the womb itself. Perhaps some of these titles, translated from some ancient tongue into Gaelic, came from Druidic times in a similar fashion to today's use of evergreen boughs, holly and mistletoe in fashion during Christian celebrations. A tiny hot fire of our past reality flickering in the heart of our present.

From where I sat looking to the north-west, I could see where the end lochan met a cluster of small knolls, and on the left of this obstruction the water had found an exit where it slipped quietly, easing its way between time-blackened stones over a sandstone apron to disappear towards the sea. I was to find that this small river had a story of its own to tell, but that lay in various tumbles through dark bedrock slides and waterfalls where the shadowed watercourses held an atmosphere of mystery.

Born on the rainbow mists of falling water, where sight dissolves in the unknown depths gouged from the mother rock, happenings of the past are shrouded in the endless crashing of water, and cadences of Gaelic voices long gone with their laughter, music and pain, all washed about in the ether of that thing we call time.

That part of the hill has since become home to me, and one day, I too will join the voices in the ether of those quiet places, to become perhaps yet another of the unknown. Those who follow, if they will, might also find the solace of soul peace if they have the time to go and absorb the quiet places through my eyes. They might remember grandparents who at last set roots in a place long settled by those who had blood knowledge of that land, as they sit on a rock and watch the first lochan which was fed by the burn from a reed bed.

The Later Years

The Colours Of A Season

Grasses glowing gently blowing, mosses green and russet brown,
In the patchwork of the moorland and the rocks that lie around,
Where the jack snipe rise to windward from the rushes beating fast,
Circling over in the heavens, dropping down to light at last.

There we wander 'midst the peat hags to the summer grazing ground,
Where the prints of roaming stag herds in the sheltered spots abound,
'Till we see them on the skyline showing darkly on the crest,
And the forest of their antlers grace the knolls on which they rest.

Smell the myrtle in the hollow 'tween our bodies and the peat,
Whilst the colours of the lichen form a rainbow at our feet.
In the shadow under boulders where the spring time violets bloom,
See the beauty of the milkwort as it helps dispel the gloom.

Ah! Those golden days of autumn, and the snow not far away
From the high tops where the eagles, and the hungry ravens play,
Where the blue hare in the hollow sits with dreamy eyes a'doze,
And the ptarmigan churrs softly as she dons her winter clothes.

We who are blessed with the ability to walk and have 'eyes to see' have a special gift wherein we can participate with nature and help nurture it. Those who cannot walk or have the blessing of sight must participate in other ways—through the eyes of others and their goodness, but we are all of the stuff of nature and thus—when we wilfully and needlessly destroy parts of it—we are unwittingly, hurting ourselves. This planet which sustains our life is not infinite in its resources but very much a finite entity.

To say that man can destroy the planet is perhaps a bit arrogant as greater forces than we can ever invent have moulded and shattered the earth, but we are possibly the most sentient and intelligent species on earth, and even more so, if we are born of the stuff of God and placed here to look after the earth, then it is our responsibility to make a much better job of it than we are doing right now.

We might not be capable of destroying the Earth, but we are certainly capable of destroying ourselves and many other living things whilst the planet would still spin and most likely evolve some species all over again.

We are as nothing.

Conservation has developed in the eyes of ordinary landworkers into a government-funded bureau for the more educated and those who serve their needs. Some well-meaning eco scientists travel down roads of thought which veer from the sublime to the ridiculous and in this the problem lies not in a lack of good intention, but in the blinkered reaction inherent in mankind where the gift of education sometimes develops an inherent platform of superiority and reacts adversely when intellectual viewpoints are challenged by plain common sense if forwarded by equally intelligent but less educated souls.

If snow habitually drifts in certain places it is because of the prevailing winds and how they behave.

Any shepherd from the area could pinpoint precisely where the drifts occur, but this is mere 'anecdotal evidence' which is unacceptable. It requires the certificated evidence of a trained engineer with a degree, and at considerable expense to the taxpayer before the facts will be accepted.

This is the division which gets in the way of progress. It is the human failing of competitive and prideful rejection towards compromise in acknowledging the worth of common-sense and experience.

The simple truth is that traditional word of mouth cannot be dismissed as 'mere anecdotal evidence aired around a bar counter', as was rather patronisingly pronounced by one 'eco-boffin' at a deer meeting where he obviously felt rather comfortable amongst his associates who were to later reveal themselves as a party to merciless deer slaughter on unfenced ground where stags had come down in the snow for succour. The accumulated experience garnered and handed down from one stalking generation to another is a valuable planetary tool which, in conjunction with new-age scientific discoveries, can achieve great benefits, but first there has to be an amicable meeting of minds.

Wild animal management and the task of tending the lands on which they live should be as sacrosanct during the relevant seasons as the office desk in a bank or the lathes in the workshops of an aerospace factory. The whole management scenario of the countryside is hindered by historical grudges inherent in class division regarding countryside pursuits but this is largely becoming obsolete and now used by those with an anarchistic intent for habitual disruption.

As in any institution, pursuit or business, there are areas where the nature of humankind has bent the rules to suit expediency, and there will always be those in the countryside, amongst landlords and the public who will imagine that they are God's gift to the planet and they have exceptional rights.

On the other hand there are private owners of large tracts of land who make excellent custodians and who are the least expensive drain on the public purse, whilst the public have, in the main, almost unlimited access to most areas.

What we require is school education regarding the real facts of our countryside and the animals therein, but in some cases, however, it has been revealed that such education is being actively barred by certain school teachers, either because of political bias or their unrealistic leanings towards Walt Disney films where animals are given human characteristics. Thus they intentionally fail in their duty to present the facts and the resulting corruption of young minds is incalculable.

But now I hope that you will sit beside me and share just a few of my memories of the times when I sat at my writing desk whilst I looked out of the window to the rough parks below in the northern summer light which lasts nearly all night.

Window Ponderings

S ince April I have been daily clearing one of our largest parks of deer. The grass therein was intended to be used for bagged silage, but the fences deteriorated to such an extent that a complete dismantling and clear out is required before any meaningful fencing can be restored. The deer have been literally, if inadvertently because of ignorance, been trained to utilise these parks, and the foolishness of the departed tenant in imagining that wild deer can be herded like sheep cannot be fathomed. Goodness knows, sheep are difficult enough in themselves, as like deer, they become hefted to an area, especially if they are born into and adopt the habit of being there.

It is now the middle of June, I have largely educated the deer into utilising the gate for entry and exit, and I hope that when the fences are once more properly raised, there will be much less marauding damage. One of three hinds was seen walking the fence this morning, with a calf trotting the other side. Three deer is quite a change from over seventy, but the hill grass has begun growing at last, and this, added to the fact that many of the hinds will have dropped their calves on the brae faces, might help to keep grass marauding to a minimum. I was admiring the darting movements of the little calf, and memories of my own youth stirred as I pondered the freshness and relatively uncomplicated process of the wild.

More From the Window

The end of June has come, and two calves have met for the first time on the woodland edge some hundred yards below our window. Their mothers are keeping an eye on things, but as long as their offspring remain in sight, they are mainly unconcerned and occupy themselves with the all-important task of feeding in order to recoup body weight and produce milk. One of the calves is a few days older than the other, and its mischievous attempts to coax the younger one to play are being interpreted with some timidity. Once they have become more used to one another the fun should begin, and no doubt by then some other newcomer will become the recipient of pecking order hoof taps and lowered butting heads. Children of all sorts have these characteristics, but these deer infants have the divine innocence first conceived as being a part of the Garden of Eden. They are fortunate in their eternal innocence.

By comparison the human species have fallen badly in their responsibilities and perhaps their assumed dominion is not as absolute or self-perpetuating as might smugly be thought. We might have a dominant place amongst the animal life on the planet, but in the light of what most humans are about, we certainly do not deserve to dominate the planet and we certainly do not own it.

From recent planetary upheavals—if anyone has taken the time to notice—a proper sense of our actual worth and false sense of impunity is being made clear, but like mindless things, the wars still go on and people amidst nature's demonstrations of cataclysmic potential, use the upheavals as an excuse to indulge in the most illegal forms of materialistic greed. I sincerely hope that the race between the application of common sense and materialism will be resolved in favour of the former before it is too late. We should be heading forward into the new millennium with an enlightened agenda, both spiritual and physical.

The Rolling Stone

I tossed a stone at a hind today
as I passed along her wandering way,
and in the peace of the passes high
she watched the stone as it rolled her by.

Her ears were cocked in gracious pose
as she followed the flight with her dewy nose,
Interested but not in fear
In the morning time of the travelling deer.

It was not hard to find a stone to toss, as two thirds of the immediate hilltops adjacent to the Bheinn 'a Bhan on Applecross seem to be comprised of bedrock in the form of Torridonian sandstone. I was endeavouring to chase the hind and her calf from the roadside without actually striking her, but for some reason she chose to exhibit absolutely no concern.

The first stone was followed by others with the same effect, and it was not until I left my van and walked over to tick her off that she about-turned and trotted away. This would have been about 1986, and I had been stalking this ground for fifteen years. I hated to disturb these animals, but trust in mankind is, for the most part, poorly placed by wild animals, and it would only be a matter of time before this lady would either get struck by a vehicle, or encounter a passing poacher's. 22 bullet placed with the aid of a lamp.

It is an unadvisable but almost inevitable trap to become emotionally involved with deer which are constantly prone to the vicissitudes of Highland weather and this is doubly so because in the eyes of the law, these deer in fact belong to no one. All management and culling systems of control are tenuous links at best if neighbouring forest owners are not of the same mind, as these animals only have to walk over a deer forest boundary in order to emerge into a totally different reality. The alternative, however, is to adopt a negative attitude and just shoot unselectively the number which one wants. We have been relatively lucky on this forest, as we are surrounded on three sides by sea. Our boundary to the neighbouring ground is marked by a long loch, and a bastion of large, steep coires which are flanked largely by boulder-strewn moon landscapes which lead down to the water. There is little—thank goodness—to attract the stags across the boundaries of that area, except perhaps winter forays across to the nearest roadside which is not on this estate, and which presents a constant danger.

Some people claim that selective shooting is a waste of time. Well it is if there is not a common understanding between adjoining forests to shoot only substandard beasts, and the animals thereon have free access between. As far as expertise goes however, there are a lot of assertive noises made by some who lay claim to special knowledge, but who are often just pushing their unsupported theories or ideas that they have chosen from selected writings, onto others without having any real long-term personal experience with which to substantiate them.

There is such a thing as literary bullying, and for those who are good with words on paper, but have the wrong motivation, it is quite easy to bulldoze through other people's legitimate opinions and feelings. It is essential to place the well-being of the deer first and keep an open mind, bearing in mind that different areas sometimes need different approaches and tactics.

The old ways and new herd management ideas all have merits and demerits, and it is important to recognise wisdom where it emerges, recognising that self-opinionated axe grinding is no substitute for plain common sense. It would be a sad mistake if every altruistic hill stalker—some with many years of hard-earned experience was called a liar by inference just because he or she operated on 'anecdotal' data and not on reams of garnered figures, or literature gained from an 'expert'.

We have seen culling activities based on annual garnered figures, overridden by authorities simply because this did not meet with quangoistic approval, and unfortunately, have also seen that the slaughter under authoritarian demands to decimate deer herds, brought them to the point where management became a farce and the shooting pressure had to be halted in order to regain some breeding stability for the future.

There are old stories about migrating deer, and of stags moving en masse from one forest to another. I have never seen or heard of this happening in my lifetime, but believe that during times of higher human population, there might have been more incentive for stags to move. I know from observation that hinds in this area are more prone to remain static, but stags are certainly liable to wander in search of females if they are not available on the ground during the rut. This is especially so if there is sufficient disturbance to encourage migration, and stags will evacuate an area altogether once disturbance has become chronic. In Coire na Ba which was always full of stags in the old days, numbers dwindled once the road became metalled and busier, and now there is a resident parcel of perhaps half a dozen visiting where once there was an established parcel of around thirty.

The same situation has developed over on the north side of the hill at Creag Gorm where we used to have a permanent summer population of twenty-five stags only half a mile away from the road. Now there are none.

Cultural Changes

By and large, the historical and musical culture of the common folk has, because there were very few people who could write, been passed down from generation to generation by word of mouth. Art forms have always been an integral part of country peoples' existence, but the written word was considered to be the prerogative of the scholar or academic. This, however, is the age of change, and it has brought about the enlightenment of unrestricted education as well as a gradual emancipation from various forms of superstition and bondage. These freedoms are, however, not always utilised in an altruistic manner.

I was sitting at four o'clock in the morning of a new June day in 1996. The light was nearly full outside, and I recalled the conversation I had with a good friend of mine several nights before. We were both acutely aware that rapid change was taking place throughout the countryside, and that things would never be the same again in our time.

Solitary places will never again be quite so solitary, and a 'packaged' form of utilitarian humanisation is invading and destroying the last bastions of the natural world where peace was once a sinecure. Animals are being ruthlessly displaced, either because they are a nuisance, or because in an inadvertent manner their territory is being increasingly disturbed by human incursion.

Nature organisations, influenced at every turn by suburban euphemistic intellect and with their diverse opinions on which creatures are of more importance, are encouraging this bureaucratisation of the remaining wild places under the trendy guise of so-called 'freedom for all' and the 'right to roam' by a rapidly-increasing population who wish to use these natural resources as a playground.

In many cases it can be seen that numbers of these people come to the countryside in order to utilise it then discard their litter as they go. They are either moronically oblivious to the pollution they create or they simply regard litter collection as someone else's responsibility.

This attitude is helping to accelerate the penetration and disruption of natural resources all over the globe and the awful truth is that this behaviour has been inadvertently sanctioned by a succession of governments who themselves appear to pay little but lip service to the planet's needs as long as the majority of voting public which dwells in suburbia has weekend countryside entertainment.

Before this age of government-encouraged intrusion exploded about the countryperson's ears the lives of most of us during the post-war years were largely governed by eking out a living as best we could from whatever could be honestly utilised. This became an ingrained habit through time, but it should never be misconstrued as meanness. Because of my habit of looking after the items I own or my ways of making, mending and re-inventing I often encounter strange looks from the New Age consumer generation, but if some calamity ever did befall us all, it is people from my reality who would furnish our shelters from scrap and bring home the meat until re-education began.

And So, To the Original Reason for Writing This Book

To our grandchildren

I leave these pages in your care for your children and grandchildren in order that they might know something of their roots.

This series of stories and experiences which have been jotted down over the years is now being compiled as I sit at my writing desk in our home at Lonbain. 'Home' is a house which I never envisaged would exist when I first sat at the end of the chain of lochans and felt inspired by the idea of writing this story. The lochans lie about a mile and a half above here just over the ridge of the hill and forty years ago when I first knew this place, it was derelict crofting land. I never then dreamed that Gwendy and I would be given a croft to rent here at last, nor that we would manage to create the modest woodland sanctuary which we now have.

In a joint effort by our eldest daughter Kathleen and ourselves, Kathleen in generously helping with vital finance over the years, and our crofting benefits including land tenure, we have created a haven in which to live whilst hopefully handing on a beautiful property to her children.

Because during our earlier lives Gwendy and I owned little but that which could be carried in a few suitcases, we have been well blessed beyond all hopes, but during our latter years here we have managed to purchase the croft. We were prompted by the knowledge that from the coastal road which passes a hundred yards above our property, acquisitive eyes began to assess what we had created out of a wilderness, and revealed an interest in shouldering us to one side.

In the November of 2001 we moved into this house which we named Tigh na Mara (House on the Sea). It was solidly built by Alan Cross who is a local builder and for the first winter we endured unending, howling winds, then one morning in February we woke up to a strange new sound—the sound of silence. The winds had gone.

Since then ten years have passed and in that time we have—along with our neighbour—instated a deer fence, and on this portion I have planted many hundreds of varied trees and hedging bushes. Some of those trees are now over fifteen feet tall and the rejuvenated herbage, cover and seeds have provided a valuable bird habitat.

Recently I was pottering about trying to find a space into which I might transplant a number of small oak trees which we have grown from acorns. I had a job on my hands simply because the sensible planting space is beginning to fill up, and there is always the worry of destructive voles, despite the hard work of our two willing feline companions, Thomas and Whiskers, and Charlie our terrier.

For those who wish to investigate in the future, however, they will find oaks which we have grown from seed garnered during our travels around various parts of France and Britain. Mountain scrub oaks included. Over ninety percent of our trees have some from seeds, cuttings and roadside ditches.

Gwendy and I are both getting older. I get around in low gear due to arthritis whilst some plumbing has been done to my heart and I have a part-diet of pills with which to keep me going. Gwendy is also a lot slower and will be investigated very soon to see if she too has angina. We worked hard at our lives and I'm afraid that I must admit to you grandchildren who will read this, that we worked your parents fairly hard as well until they finished their education and spread their wings with our blessing in order to leave home. There were times when they probably had little to thank us for, but you have parents who have the ability to cater well on very little, are able to make and mend, and have demonstrated a capacity for high intelligence and hard work.

So, from these beginnings of four generations you have been launched into a more progressive world in order that you might, hopefully, never know hard times despite the honey-coated traps of modern life which lie in wait.

You should have no need to live for weeks on fried oatmeal and onions, or survive on snared rabbit cooked up with some skirt of beef for taste and nutrition (as rabbit provides very little). Nor will you sup on soup made from half a sheep's head along with some vegetables, the head which was chopped in half after being singed with a red-hot iron on a wooden chopping block outside the local butcher's shop, or have to run home starving in the late summer's evening with dried trout hanging off a forked twig after catching them in various river pools miles from home.

But with those memories, perhaps I am the luckiest as I have lived a very full and rich life. From the experiences and our way of living your grandmother and I have met-with and made some gifted, generously unique and loving friends from all stations in life.

Of your own forebears; first there were the amazingly hardy generations of great-great-grandparents and great-grandparents handed on from Victorian times—the former who participated in the bloodbath of the First Great War and the latter in the Second World War. They were unaware of the backroom politics, the secret reasons for politicians sending good people to be slaughtered on their behalf. They were sometimes aware however, of the lately revealed idiocies by those in command who at times sent valuable men to be slaughtered like animals because of an arrogant whim, and if they refused, would be shot at the stake as cowards.

No. The reason your forefathers fought was because they were informed, and believed that their future freedom, and that of their descendants—myself, you, and your children—was at stake, so they journeyed through the gates of fear and hell in order to ensure that we all had the freedom which we enjoy today. Please never forget them.

Then there was the generation of grandparents who include Gwendy and I, who went on from there to improve on that which was handed to them, albeit some of us still handicapped during the earlier years by poor wages.

This was followed by the generation of your parents who were launched into a New Age of freedom away from dingy-coloured clothing and with an amazing world of fresh ideas, freedom of thought and new technology which, through hard work they have grasped and handed on to you.

You are the future. Remember what you came from and be resolved. You will probably witness amazing things beyond our imagining.

The end.
Or is it a new beginning?

Lightning Source UK Ltd.
Milton Keynes UK
UKOW031459221211

184253UK00001B/21/P